With
Colorful
Regards, Jan!

Ann Marbury
11/17/95

THE POWER OF
COLOR

THE POWER OF
COLOR

Creating Healthy Interior Spaces

Sara O. Marberry
Laurie Zagon

John Wiley & Sons, Inc.

New York   Chichester   Brisbane   Toronto   Singapore

Copyright © 1995 by John Wiley & Sons, Inc.

Library of Congress Cataloging in Publication Data:

Marberry, Sara O., 1959–
    The power of color: creating healthy interior spaces / by Sara O.
  Marberry and Laurie Zagon.
      p. cm. — (Construction business and management library)
      Includes bibliographical references (p.   ) and index.
      ISBN 0-471-07685-6 (alk. paper)
      1. Color in interior decoration. 2. Public buildings —Decoration—
  United States. 3. Color—Health aspects. I. Zagon, Laurie.
  II. Title. III. Series.
    NK2195.P8M37 1995
    729—dc20   94-23831

Printed in the United States of America

10 9 8 7 6 5 4 3 2 1

CONTENTS

Preface   vii

Acknowledgments   xi

1 COLOR THEORY
REVISITED   2

2 COLOR AS
LIGHT AND ENERGY   10

3 USING FULL-SPECTRUM COLOR
IN INTERIOR SPACES   18

4 PROJECT EXAMPLES:
HOSPITALITY, LABORATORIES, OFFICES, SCHOOLS   26

5 PROJECT EXAMPLES:
HEALTHCARE   34

POSTSCRIPT   45

Appendix:
THE DESIGN OF HEALING ENVIRONMENTS
by Jain Malkin   79

CHAPTER REFERENCES AND SOURCES   93

FURTHER READING   101

INDEX   109

PREFACE

This book was born out of a need in the worlds of design and health to understand color as architectural form—not solely as decoration—and to understand color as energy. Color is a life force that *is* light. It is made up of electromagnetic wavelengths that can be measured by frequency. The more powerful the frequency, the more powerful the color. Since such frequencies can be measured on any surface or object, it is possible for design professionals to use color in a systematic and sensible order based on the laws of nature.

We believe that when this natural order of color is used in the design of interior spaces, a harmonious sensation occurs, which, in turn, positively affects the health and well-being of those interacting with the space. If color is used strictly as one person's random choices for decoration, a feeling of imbalance can result. In some cases, people may feel physical discomfort from this dissonance of color, and at other times they may simply feel emotionally upset.

Each of us belongs to the same universe that is in a natural state of balance. This inherent order of things carries over to all aspects of our lives. When there is not enough light, we turn on a lamp. Similarly, we can also "turn on" more color, in whatever dosages of intensities or neutralities are necessary. Not all of us require the same dosages of color, and we each have a personal color palette.

In creating healthy interior spaces, these personal color palettes should not interfere with the universal system of color. They should be separate from the color palettes we choose for general public spaces. Evaluating what is needed in terms of color for commercial interiors is best analyzed by first identifying the needs of the people who will be interacting with such spaces. If a quiet, meditative area is required, then a soft, neutralized palette using a progression of primary and secondary colors might be appropriate.

Colors in harmony are like music—there are as many variations of style in music as there are in color harmony. As in music, there are notes ranging in scales, just as there are scales of color, that is, the value and chroma scales outlined in Chapter 1 of this book. This flow of scales creates the natural rhythm of color palettes in interior spaces. In an area in which people need a fair amount of stimulation, such as a long-term care facility for older people, the "sounds" of color might be pure, bold primary reds, yellows, and blues to help with wayfinding or to generate additional energy.

We believe that, in order to reach the harmonious goal of using color as form, it is important to create a structure of color that has a systematic progression of change. The best way for professionals to accomplish this is to study color theory systems and apply the appropriate structure, using the entire range of the color spectrum.

We also believe that interior design is an art and that the creative process of designing interior space in many ways parallels painting and sculpture. The expression of color in interior spaces is part of the designer's artistic statement. It is an instinctual process that need not become bogged down in theory but, by following a few simple guidelines, can make the difference between good and great design.

Chapter 1 of this book is a basic refresher course in color theory principles and techniques for the professional. This chapter is a tool for understanding the infrastructure of full-spectrum color, which is, in fact, color theory. Chapter 2 investigates color as light and reveals more information than has been previously compiled in one book on the use of color for healing. Chapter 3 further explains surface colors and lighting, how to use full-spectrum color in interior design, and why it is so important.

Chapters 4 and 5 describe and evaluate commercial projects from across the United States (as well as one from Europe), designed by talented professionals who, intentionally or not, incorporated a full-spectrum color palette. Various uses of full-spectrum color are shown in these projects, ranging from the bright primary look, a more grayed-to-brown neutralized palette, to a more pastel range with an obvious sensation of each of the primary and secondary colors. Photos of these projects are shown in the Project Showcase starting on page 47.

Finally, a Postscript offers some thoughts on what we see as the next steps for color in design, as well as recommended actions. The Further Reading section provides a list of recommended books, plus articles and papers describing the best documented research on color response, light, and health that we could find. For the Appendix, we include a paper written by Jain Malkin on healing environments because, although it focuses on healthcare, we feel that it best describes what constitutes healthy interior spaces.

We chose to write about this topic because both of our careers over the past 20 years have focused on color and, more recently, its health implications and applications. We have created this book as a tool for all who are involved in the decision-making process to create healthy interior spaces. We hope it will provide a new language, methodology, and dialogue on color between the designer and the client. Because of format constraints, we were unable to include residential spaces in our analysis of projects, but we encourage the use of full-spectrum color principles in those spaces as well.

As we researched material for this book, we were reminded that most of the data available on color is out-of-date. There are, however, many people interested in having access to this type of research. Therefore, though we acknowledge that it is difficult to measure, the need for *new research* in the area of the physiological healing effects of color is most urgent.

We hope that this book will stimulate interest and generate support for further research on this very important subject.

Sara O. Marberry
Laurie Zagon
September 1994

ACKNOWLEDGMENTS

The authors would like to acknowledge the following people for their contributions to and support of this book:

- Amanda Miller, editor, John Wiley & Sons
- Wayne Ruga, president and CEO, The Center for Health Design
- Jain Malkin, president, Jain Malkin Inc.
- Kerwin Kettler, former academic dean, New York School of Interior Design
- All of the design professionals and photographers whose work appears in Chapters 4 and 5

Sara Marberry would like to dedicate this book to the following individuals:

- My husband, Richard Marberry, for his loving support and continuing encouragement
- Wayne Ruga, my friend and colleague, who has always challenged me to go the extra mile
- Jim Bidwill, senior vice president, Merchandise Mart Properties, my very first mentor who introduced me to the world of interior design

Laurie Zagon would like to dedicate this book to the following individuals:

- My wonderful and loving husband, Joe Sorrentino, who inspired me to research the industrial aspects of color related to health
- Cheryl Woodruff, senior editor, Ballantine, for being the first person to publish my work
- Robert Fritz, an incredible teacher and important creative force in my life
- The late Reba Stewart, my mentor and professor of color theory (who had studied with Josef Albers at Yale) at the Maryland Institute College of Art, who encouraged me as an artist and colorist

ACKNOWLEDGMENTS

- The late Professors Herbert Aach and Helen Schiavo, who both made the decision to hire me—23 years old and right out of graduate school—from among 100 professional applicants, to teach color theory at the City University of New York/Queens College
- All the students who have taught me as much, if not more, than I have taught them

THE POWER OF
COLOR

1

COLOR
THEORY
REVISITED

To fully understand the concept of using full-spectrum color in interior spaces, it is helpful first to review basic color theory principles. Many books have been written that present these principles in great detail, but most are scientific in nature and require intense study to comprehend. The serious student of color will want to read and study these books, but practicing design professionals and facility planners need only a working knowledge to achieve good results when using color in interior spaces.

From a historical perspective, the development of color theory as an educational course in the analysis of color and form in nature began in 1919 when Wassily Kandinsky, the renowned Russian abstract artist and teacher, was appointed to the faculty of the Bauhaus School of Design in Weimar, Germany. This school became famous throughout the world for revolutionizing the teaching of architecture, industrial arts, painting, and sculpture. The collaborative efforts of the faculty made this school unique in its teachings. Faculty members also included artist Paul Klee, artist/color theorist Johannes Itten, and the Bauhaus founder, architect Walter Gropius. This group of colleagues often discussed the importance of nature study in terms of the seasonal systems of color change. They agreed that the infinite asymmetrical and symmetrical color relationships apparent in nature offered an orderly system for the study of color and design. The enormous spiritual inspiration also gained from nature created a counterpart to this new way of teaching.

Early color theory principles came from these important teaching collaborations at the Bauhaus School. Itten developed the first basic course on form and color. He ultimately devoted five decades to the visual, psychological, and esthetic mysteries of color. After leaving the Bauhaus, he directed his own school in Berlin from 1924 to 1934, where he authored *Design and Form*, derived from the basic course he originated at the Bauhaus, and expanded his color theories through the creation and exhibition of his paintings. To further investigate all aspects of color interaction, he studied the scientific color studies and charts of Goethe, the systems of music explained by the German composer Schopenhauer, and the complementary color relationships of the French colorist and textile designer Chevreul.

Itten's most famous work, *The Elements of Color,* originally published in German in 1961 under the title *Kunst der Farbe,* and later in English in 1970, is still the most widely used book by colleges and universities that offer a course in color theory principles. What makes

4

The Elements of Color a great learning tool for students learning about color is its readability. Over the years, color theory principles have not changed; they have only been redefined. The sign of a great teacher is his or her ability to present information clearly and succinctly. Itten's book is easy to understand because it offers short and explicit descriptions of the basic color combinations and has simple color charts that usually restate his writing. He often said, "He who wants to become a master of color must see, feel, and experience each individual color in its many endless combinations with all colors."

One of Itten's most notable students was Josef Albers, who entered the Bauhaus School as a student in 1920. His work with colored glass assemblage was so highly respected that in 1922 he was asked to teach a glass workshop. In 1923 he was asked by Gropius to teach the basic design class. Albers remained at the Bauhaus School throughout its term and left when it closed in 1933.

In 1933, Albers came to the United States with his wife, artist/weaver Anni Albers, to teach at Black Mountain College in North Carolina (a school from which many abstract expressionist artists, including Jackson Pollock and Helen Frankenthaler, emerged) along with his colleague, the German abstract colorist Hans Hoffman. It was at Black Mountain College that these renowned artists explored color relationships without a representational object-oriented structure. They used the simplicity of color to create form instead of the traditional still life, landscape, or figure format, a movement later referred to as "abstract expressionism."

Albers began his most notable work on color in 1949 and taught at Yale University from 1950 to 1960. His work on the illusion of color and light on a two-dimensional surface became his focus through the famous "Homage to the Square" series.

Albers was responsible for introducing the first color theory course in the United States at Yale. Many famous artists who studied at Yale in the 1950s implemented his color principles. Through their teachings, these artists subsequently brought the color theory course to many university art and design programs throughout the country. Albers's book, *Interaction of Color,* published by Yale University Press in 1963, capsulized a decade of work with his students. It showed the effects of simultaneous contrast by revealing the changing effects of a color resulting from its relationship with a background color environment.

Albers became well known for his color teaching by developing extensive numbers of subtractive color mixtures and then hand silk-screening the inks onto white papers. The students would cut the colored papers into squares (as large as 8 by 10 inches) and then cut small 2-inch squares of different colors. The smaller squares were placed on the larger ones so that the students could see the effect of their interactions with the background colors. This was the basis for Albers's extensive study of simultaneous contrast. He felt that by using silk-screen inks, the students could see that color had no surface interference and could be used for mixing modulations of color. The screen inks dried fast on paper, and the finished colored papers could be shared by several students for color study.

One of Albers's students was later responsible for manufacturing similar silk-screened colored papers and developing them into a product known as Color-Aid paper. Many university color theory courses recommend that students purchase a box of Color-Aid papers to enhance their study of color.

COLOR THEORY PRINCIPLES

These well-known artists and colorists capsulized the two basic color systems that form the foundation for basic color theory principles. The first is the additive system, which is a mixing of light that involves combining red, green, and blue to make white light. This is founded on the principles of Sir Isaac Newton's bent-prism experiments that revealed the existence of the rainbow.

The second is the subtractive system, which physically mixes red, yellow, and blue pigments to make near black. The main difference between the two systems is that in the additive system, the spectrum is made up of seven colors: red, orange, yellow, green, blue, indigo, and violet. In the subtractive system—owing to the fact that we are working with man-made pigments—all the physical mixtures used are based on the primary and secondary colors of red, orange, yellow, green, blue, and violet, with the absence of indigo. Indigo, actually the perfect mixture of blue and violet, can be mixed in the subtractive system by combining those two colors.

6

The mixture of pigments in the subtractive system is the most helpful in understanding the interaction of colors in interior spaces, which is based on the systems, structures, and patterns of colors as seen in nature. A rainbow of light would not be the same if one of the seven colors were missing. The elimination of just one hue would change the natural structure of the rainbow and throw off the refraction of its consecutive system.

The same is true when a hue is deleted in interior design. When the primary colors of red, yellow, and blue and the secondary colors of orange, green, and violet are arranged in a consecutive circular order, a continuous flow of harmony is apparent (see color plates, Figure 1). The primary colors are known as a major triad, and the secondary colors as a minor triad (see the chart below). From these triads are derived many color harmonies. The harmonies are produced by grouping colors to create a balance of color as recognized in nature.

The most common color harmonies are as follows:

- *Analogous harmony*—colors next to each other on the wheel (see the chart on the opposite page).
- *Complementary harmony*—colors opposite each other on the wheel (see the chart on the opposite page).
- *Split complement harmony*—two directly opposite colors, along with one or two more that are analogous to one or the other, or both.
- *Full-spectrum harmony*—all colors, used in varied proportions, values, and chroma changes.

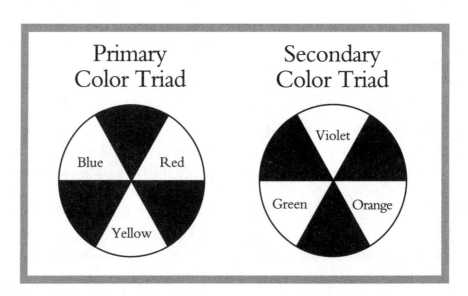

Primary Color Triad

Secondary Color Triad

Analogous Hues

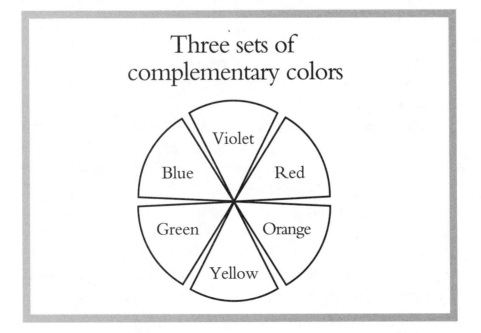

Yellow Orange · Yellow · Yellow Green
Orange Yellow · Green Yellow
Orange · Green
Orange Red · Green Blue
Red Orange · Blue Green
Red · Blue
Red Violet · Blue Violet
Violet Red · Violet Blue
Violet

Three sets of complementary colors

Violet

Blue · Red

Green · Orange

Yellow

8

The basic understanding of all color theory relies on three simple categories: hue, value, and chroma. *Hue* is a designated color derived from one of the primaries (red, yellow, blue) or secondaries (orange, green, violet). *Value* is defined as the lightness and darkness of a hue (tints and shades). *Chroma* is best defined as the brilliance, intensity, or saturation of a given hue.

For example, primary red is a hue. Primary red pigment with white added makes a value of red (tint), which is pink. The same red pigment with black added makes a value of red (shade), which is burgundy.

Primary red by itself is the highest intensity red, which makes it a high-chroma, extemely brilliant red. The same red mixed with its opposite of primary green in near equal proportions produces the lowest intensity of red—low chroma—which is an extremely gray neutral.

These three elements—hue, value, and chroma—when paired in various positions create seven color contrasts. These seven contrasts, as described by Itten, are as follows:

1. **Contrast of hue.** Occurs when two different hues, such as primary red and primary green, are placed together.
2. **Contrast of light and dark.** Occurs when lights and darks (tints and shades), such as charcoal and pink, are used together.
3. **Contrast of cold and warm.** Occurs when two colors of different temperatures, such as orange (warm) and blue (cool), are placed together.
4. **Contrast of complements.** Occurs when two colors that are opposite each other on the color wheel, such as violet and yellow, are used together.
5. **Contrast of simultaneity.** Occurs when one color is placed on two different backgrounds, the color will appear to have two identities, thus producing a contrast. A small blue square on a green background and the same blue square on a red background will appear to be two different blues.
6. **Contrast of saturation.** Occurs when two colors with different intensities, such as electric blue and neutral blue–gray, are used together.
7. **Contrast of extension.** Occurs when colors are placed together in different proportions, such as the three pairs of complements in the following ratios: red and green at 1/2 : 1/2; violet and yellow at

9

$1/4 : 3/4$; and blue and orange at $1/3 : 2/3$. This also applies to the circle of primary and secondary colors in harmonious proportion.

BLACK AND WHITE

The use of black and white in interiors creates the feeling of dark and light contrast. Black is mixed by blending the major triad of red, yellow, and blue. Black can create a sense of drama and shadow, but too much black can produce an overall sense of depression and despair because of the lack of light.

White, on the other hand, is the *absence* of color in the subtractive mixture system, and *all* colors in the additive system of mixing red, green, and blue. When used in interior spaces, white creates a feeling of luminosity and clarity. Coupled with a full-spectrum color palette, white separates space and enhances the eye's ability to focus.

Gray, a combination of black and white, is a great neutralizer of space. The French Impressionist painters often used neutral grays with higher-intensity triad colors. They felt that the combination of the neutrals with other colors created a jewel-like effect. They also felt that their work had a greater harmony when the absence of black was compensated for by the use of neutrals (mixing of complementary pairs of colors) or near black (mixing primary colors).

SUMMARY

When planning interior spaces, it is important to understand these basic color principles so that color can be used to create form, rather than used only as decoration. Using balanced proportions of the entire spectrum in a systematic order provides a natural harmony that many experts feel can promote health and well-being. When colors are chosen personally or randomly, an uneasy, lifeless, or even chaotic effect often results. The overall success of a design scheme can be undermined by the lack of full-spectrum balance.

The next chapter discusses the meaning of full-spectrum color, as well as how best it can be used to create healthy interior spaces.

2

COLOR AS LIGHT AND ENERGY

Let us begin with the premise that color and light are synonymous. There cannot be one without the other. This principle was initially discovered in 1672 by Sir Isaac Newton when he experimented with passing sunlight through a glass prism. He found that when a beam of white light is passed through a prism, it splits into a rainbow revealing seven visible colors: red, orange, yellow, green, blue, indigo, and violet.

All living things—people, plants, and animals—need light to thrive. For many animals, systems of light are particularly important because their bodily functions are contingent on their synchronicity to nature. Behavioral patterns, such as hibernation and breeding, are dictated by seasonal changes. People's reactions are influenced in a similar fashion.

In his book, *Light Medicine of the Future,* noted optometrist Jacob Liberman explains how light enters the body through the eyes: "The pineal gland is located deep in the center of the brain between the two hemispheres and behind and above the pituitary gland. Although it is only the size of a pea, its functions are vast. It acts as the body's light meter, receiving light-activated information from the eyes (by way of the hypothalamus) and then sending out hormonal messages that have a profound effect on the mind and body."

The powerful hormone melatonin, manufactured by the pineal gland in the eyes, regulates the body's daily rhythm and functions. Light, in effect, activates our biological clock. Melatonin is released in response to darkness during the sleep cycle. Without the influence of light on the body, our rhythmic functions would be highly undisciplined. Clearly, the sun is the master of all these rhythms.

LIGHT HEALS

Circadian rhythms—which pertain to or designate the vital processes in plants, animals, and human beings that recur every 24 hours—prove how greatly affected we are by night and day. At Stanford University Hospital in Palo Alto, California, nature photographer Joey Fischer used a concept of visual therapy to compensate for the lack of windows in an intensive care unit (ICU). He designed a "window" that is actually a photograph of a nature scene, lighted from the back with 108 tiny computer-operated bulbs. The backlighting generates a facsimile of the different times of day, which helps patients to reestablish their normal daily cycles. In a video shown at the Third Symposium on Healthcare Design, Jeffrey Rich, M.D. of Stanford Medical Center,

remarked, "From a medical standpoint, patients tend to get very depressed if they lose their orientation to day and night, and the end result of the depression is something called 'ICU psychosis' where there's a profound disorientation."

"We feel here, as others do around the world, that when patients develop this orientation, their health is jeopardized by it."

Many studies have shown the positive healing effects of light on humans. In 1979, Fritz Hollwich, an ophthalmologist who has studied blind patients and those with cataracts before and after surgery, concluded that the absence of light, partially or totally, creates a significant upset in the physiological and emotional stability of humans.

In his pioneering book, *The Principles of Light and Color,* nineteenth-century educator and researcher Edwin Babbit documented case studies by physicians to prove his theory that all human ailments can be cured with colored light. He believed that people, plants, and animals are made up of components that have color associations and can be treated accordingly. "The trinity of colors, the red, the yellow and blue, finds representation in the three great elements of hydrogen, carbon, and oxygen, which constitute so much of the world, including the whole or large portion of the sugars, gums, starches, ethers, alcohols, many acids and much of the substance of the vegetable world," he wrote.

The effect of full-spectrum lighting on schoolchildren was documented by John Ott, M.D., in a study he conducted with the Environmental Health and Light Research Institute in 1973. Four first-grade classrooms in Sarasota, Florida, were studied: two with full-spectrum, radiation-shielded fluorescent light fixtures; and two with standard cool-white fluorescent light fixtures. All four classrooms were windowless and, except for the lighting, identical. Concealed time-lapse cameras were installed for documentation. Ott found that in the cool-white classrooms, hyperactivity, fatigue, irritability, and attentional deficits were common. In the full-spectrum classrooms, he observed marked academic improvement and positive changes in behavior within one month of the lighting installation.

Other documented cases of doctors and scientists demonstrate that inadequate or total absence of light will create bodily malfunctions. Viruses causing AIDS have been treated with light therapy (photodynamic therapy) by scientists at the Baylor University Medical

Center under the direction of Lester Matthews, M.D., director of the Baylor Research Foundation. Among the other illnesses that were isolated and destroyed with the use of red light are herpes simplex (type 1—cold sores), measles, and AIDS.

Experiments have proven that properly timed exposure to light affects people's mood, performance, and the hours when they sleep and wake. According to a 1992 article in *The New York Times Good Health Magazine,* $15.5 million was spent on light therapy experiments in the United States by the National Institute of Mental Health in 1991.

It is fairly well known that light therapy can be successful in treating Seasonal Affective Disorder (SAD), a clinical form of depression that may afflict as much as 6 percent of the people in the northern areas of the United States during the winter. Other experiments have led to further discoveries. "Less familiar is growing evidence that exposure to certain intensities of light at particular times of day and for particular durations can cure some kinds of insomnia, make night workers more productive and improve the body's immune function," the article stated.

This article also reported that the National Aeronautics and Space Administration (NASA) has found that a "light therapy regimen works better than sleeping pills in helping astronauts rest during the day and stay alert at night."

Charles A. Czeisler, M.D., a pioneer in the research of circadian and sleep disorder medicine at Brigham and Women's Hospital in Boston and an associate professor of medicine at Harvard Medical School, was the first to show that artificial light can reset a person's biological clock. Psychiatrist Daniel F. Kripke at the University of California, San Diego, found that abnormally long menstrual cycles of women could be normalized by exposure to a 100-watt incandescent light.

TYPES OF LIGHT

Visible light is but a small part of the electromagnetic spectrum; in fact, it covers only 1/60 of the known radio spectrum of wavelengths.

Long waves are used for radio communication, induction heat, and photography, in which they can penetrate great distances and take pic-

tures of places or things that the human eye can barely see. Radiant heat, such as a laser beam, can measure several thousand feet from end to end.

X-rays, gamma rays, and cosmic rays are at the far and short ends of the spectrum. Most of these pass through the human body rather harmlessly, although overexposure to X-rays, laser rays, and microwaves can be dangerous and sometimes lethal. Visible light also penetrates into animal and human muscle and, if the light intensity is strong enough, into the internal organs.

As Babbit knew, people and animals also emit light and radiations of their own. This phenomenon has been demonstrated by the technique of corona discharge photography, commonly known as Kirlian photography. Semyon Kirlian was the Russian electrician who, in the 1950's, first used the technique of corona discharge photography on living organisms. In *Rainbows of Life,* Stanley Krippner, M.D., and Mikol Davis, M.D., described corona discharge photography as follows: "The device typically used in corona discharge photography consists of a flat metal plate with film positioned on its top. An object is placed on the film, and high-voltage electricity, at very low amperage, is pulsed through the metal plate. The electricity passes through the film and exposes it, producing an outline of the object on the plate as well as a surrounding corona. If the film is color sensitive, the corona discharge appears to contain a variety of color."

Kirlian's corona discharge photographs showing the "colors" of leaves, insects, animals, and human beings was documented in a 1961 report coauthored by his wife, Valentina Kirlian, in the Russian *Journal of Scientific and Applied Photography*. Their research suggested that certain sections of the body emit certain colors when they are healthy, and certain colors when they are damaged or ill. Contemporary design professionals have interpreted and used this information in various ways. In his book, *In My Room,* designer Antonio Torrice wrote, "Among other things, what [Kirlian photography] proved was the skin's absorption of light in much the same way as Newton's prism of bent light. Interestingly, as their work evolved, the Kirlians uncovered more of the body's color mystery, this time dealing with damaged organs. What I ascertained was an association between such organs and the wavelengths of light normally absorbed by them."

HOW WE SEE COLOR

The human eye visually interprets light rays (electromagnetic energy) by an interaction of the optic nerves with the brain. There are cones and rods in the retina of the eye that help distinguish dark and light, as well as color brilliance. The seven colors of the spectrum are produced by light waves of varied lengths that reflect off tangible animate and inanimate objects. Thus, these objects are not actually of a fixed physical color. Instead, they project color because light is reflected from their surfaces. Leaves on plants, for instance, appear green because they reflect green rays and absorb all other light. If a green leaf is held under red light, it would appear black. Tangible animate and inanimate objects possess all the colors of the spectrum. Therefore, whether objects are seen as colorful depends on their ability to absorb and reflect rays of light.

Colors also differ in hue, which helps us to define the difference between red and green, blue and orange, or violet and yellow. Moreover, colors differ in value and intensity. This too depends on the amount of light an object is able to reflect, or on the purity of the color, which relates to the amount of grayness in the hue. Surfaces that absorb all the light rays and reflect none appear black. Surfaces capable of reflecting all light appear red in red light; blue in blue light; and white in daylight.

Adding white to a standard hue creates a tint of that hue; for instance, adding white to red creates pink, or a tint of red. Adding black to red creates burgundy, or a shade of red; darker shades of other hues can be created in a similar way.

Human beings also see afterimages of colors. In his book, *The Principles of Harmony and the Contrast of Colors,* M.E. Chevreul, the nineteenth-century French designer and color mentor of the French Impressionists, first described this phenomenon. When seeing a primary, such as red, the human eye automatically seeks its opposite color, in this case green. A simple afterimage test can be accomplished by looking at a red square on a projection screen for 30 seconds, then immediately looking at a totally white screen. When the white screen appears, the human eye will see an afterimage of green. This is due to the fact that, by seeing only red, the eye is fatigued. To compensate for the fatigue, the eye produces green.

HUMAN RESPONSE TO COLOR

The most common associations and known responses of humans to color are the following:

- *Red*—Its nature symbol is the earth; it is defined often by its qualities of high energy and passion. Studies have shown that red has the ability to excite and raise blood pressure.
- *Orange*—Its nature symbol is the sunset; it is defined often by its qualities of emotion, expression, and warmth. Orange is noted for its ability to encourage verbal expression of emotions.
- *Yellow*—Its nature symbol is the sun; it is defined often by its qualities of optimism, clarity, and intellect. Bright yellow is often noted for its mood-enhancing ability. Yellow must be carefully applied in certain settings, as it may connote aging and the yellow skin tones associated with jaundice.
- *Green*—Its nature symbol is growth—grass and trees—and it is often defined by its qualities of nurturing, healing, and unconditional love. Because it is the opposite to red on the visual spectrum, green is often thought of as a healer of blood.
- *Blue*—Its nature symbols are the sky and the ocean; it is defined often by its qualities of relaxation, serenity, and loyalty. It is known to lower blood pressure. Blue is excellent as a healing color for nervous disorders, and because of its temperature being cool, blue is also good for relieving headaches, bleeding, open wounds, and so on.
- *Indigo*—Its nature symbol is the sunset; it is defined often by its qualities of meditation and spirituality in that it is the exact mixture of blue and violet.
- *Violet*—Its nature symbol is the violet flower; it is defined by its qualities of spirituality. Violet is also a stress reducer and can create feelings of inner calm.

SUMMARY

Color and light are synonymous, as originally proven by Sir Isaac Newton's prism experiment in 1672. Light is the essence of all living

things. Through light entering the portals of our eyes, we are continually given unconscious instructions from our masterful source of energy, the sun. This amazing power proves every day that it is in control of our lives through the natural wonder of day and night (light and dark).

All of the seven colors of the visible light spectrum need to be present to create a "facsimile" of light. These colors have electromagnetic energy that will produce healing effects similar to those of sunlight. When used to supplement daylight or other light in interior spaces, color can contribute to our health and well-being. The following chapters discuss the factors that influence our color experience and how the power of color can be effectively harnessed.

3

USING FULL-SPECTRUM COLOR IN INTERIOR SPACES

A full-spectrum color palette does not refer just to the use of bright colors in large proportions throughout a space, although this is certainly one means of achieving it. A more subtle approach is to use a balanced mix of various proportions of tints and shades from the hues of each of the seven colors of the spectrum (red, orange, yellow, green, blue, indigo, and violet).

In choosing a full-spectrum color palette, it is important to understand the significance of the proper proportions of color, as based on the seven color contrasts described in Chapter 1. Contrast of extension, in which colors are placed together in different proportions (such as the three pairs of complements in the following ratios: red and green at $1/2:1/2$; violet and yellow at $1/4:3/4$; and blue and orange at $1/3:2/3$) is particularly meaningful to the design of interior spaces.

To introduce the notion of a full-spectrum color palette to clients or staff members, some simple painting exercises may be helpful:

- Using a water-based paint kit (which can be purchased at minimal cost from an art supply store) that contains each of the seven colors of the spectrum, have people think of an interior space (it might be an office, a lobby, a patient room, a classroom, or a hotel bedroom) and ask them to do an abstract painting using only three colors of the spectrum. Tell them that it is OK to mix the colors and give them a time limit (10 minutes) to complete the exercise.
- Ask the participants to do another painting, using all seven colors of the spectrum. Have them display their paintings and talk about why they used the colors they did. Encourage the group to display the paintings and discuss their significance.

These exercises may also provide insight into a client's color preference. Most important, it will allow clients and staff to explore their own color sensibilities and gain a greater understanding of the meaning of a full-spectrum color palette.

SELECTING APPROPRIATE FINISHES

Since every inanimate object projects color through light reflecting off its surface, it is important to remember that every surface material and finish in an interior space is part of the full-spectrum color palette. Walls, ceilings, doors, floors, woodwork, metals, furniture, fabric, windowcoverings, artwork, accessories, plants, and so forth, all contribute

to the color scheme. And do not forget about people—their skin tones, hair colors, and clothes also bring color to interior spaces.

Assuming that a full-spectrum palette is to be used, deciding on the correct proportions of color tints and shades from the color wheel of hues in an interior space totally depends on the desired effect. If the intention is to make a bold statement with color, then use of bright colors on large surfaces, such as walls, ceilings, and doors, may be appropriate. If one color is preferred over others, a full-spectrum color palette can be constructed by using the preferred color on larger surfaces and smaller proportions of the other six spectral colors in fabrics, carpeting, artwork, and accessories; or in details such as door jambs, window frames, and hardware.

Even a so-called neutral palette can be achieved by using a full-spectrum approach to color selection. One strategy is to use a neutral, such as gray or off-white, as a backdrop and introduce other color through a few selected accessories or artwork. Another method is to select a balanced palette of subdued hues that appear grayish, tannish, or brownish (such as red-brown, yellowish taupe, and gray-blue) and use them in equal proportions in materials and finishes. This will create a full-spectrum neutral palette.

Existing spaces can be converted to full-spectrum-palette easily and inexpensively by using these same principles.

Subtle paint mixes, such as those developed by New York paint consultants Donald Kaufman and Taffy Dahl, can also be used to achieve full-spectrum effects. As illustrated in their book, *Natural Palettes for Painted Rooms,* Kaufman and Dahl often combine colors to create various patinas and spectral effects.

Major laminate producers, such as Avonite, Formica, and Wilsonart, have extensive color palettes, including "faux" finishes that offer unlimited possibilities in surface materials. Fiber producers, such as Allied, BASF, DuPont, and Monsanto, use full-spectrum colors in thread construction for carpets and fabrics.

Vidarkliniken, a healing center in an anthroposophical community in Jarna, Sweden, designed by Erik Asmussen (see the analysis in Chapter 5 and Figures 37 and 38), is one of the few examples of a facility that uses surface color as part of the healing process. "Health, according to anthroposophy, is a dialectical process of balancing one-sided tendencies toward 'sclerosis,' or excessive hardening or building

up ('cold' illnesses), and 'inflammation,' or dissolution and breaking down ('warm' illnesses)," wrote Gary and Susanne Coates of the University of Kansas in a study on the building.

Based on this philosophy, Vidarkliniken's interior spaces are painted using the "lazur" method. Paint is applied in several thin, transparent layers to create a soft luminosity. According to the Coateses, colors in patient rooms are made of vegetable dyes in a casein and beeswax medium in either cool blue and blue-violet or warm rose hues. Depending on the type of illness and stage of the healing process, Vidarkliniken physicians can prescribe either warm or cool colored rooms.

Paints made with mineral dyes are used in corridors, which are a warm yellow-ochre. The exterior building color, rose-pink, is made from artificial pigments. "The result is a progression of color quality from hard to soft as one moves from outside to inside," the Coateses wrote. "The colors of the most intimate and vulnerable spaces, the patient rooms, are the softest and most alive."

In designing interior spaces, one of the most common mistakes, in relation to the imbalance of the spectrum, is to use too much yellow. For example, brass is frequently incorporated into railings, door frames, and industrial fittings and used with wood built-ins and floors in commercial interiors. Unfortunately, all these materials are of a yellow-based hue, which is the one color most associated with the yellowing or aging of the skin.

The yellow in brass and wood is not the brilliant sunshine yellow associated with a feeling of optimism and lightness. Quite the contrary, the neutrality (grayness or dullness of the yellow hue in these fixtures) will deflect the light and prevent its being at maximum intensity and offset the palette with a heaviness of yellow.

To add to this common problem, incandescent lighting (which is yellow based) is often allowed to further dominate the color palette. It is important to remember that the major triad of red, yellow, and blue provides the overall balance to a full-spectrum palette. Compensating with an excess of red and blue tones will counterbalance the ill effects of the yellow.

If incandescent lighting is permanent and cannot be changed, an infusion of yellow's opposite—violet, blue violet, or a split complement—will make a significant difference.

IMPORTANCE OF FULL-SPECTRUM LIGHTING

Proper color rendition in interior spaces is important to creating a balanced full-spectrum palette. Light quality can be objectively measured with the color rendering index (CRI), which designates 100 for incandescent light—regarded by lighting experts as the reference standard for a "natural" appearance. However, as mentioned earlier, because incandescent lamps are yellow based, they do not seem to provide a good spectral balance when used by themselves. Moreover, the color temperature of the lamp (which refers to the relative spectral balance of light wavelengths) must also be considered. A lamp at the warm end of the color temperature scale can enhance a full-spectrum palette.

Color reflections from surfaces also act as secondary light sources in interior spaces. An overuse of white or pastels can cause glare, because these colors reflect light; overuse of black or darker colors can reduce contrast, because these colors absorb light. The best strategy is a balanced use of full-spectrum color with light from additional sources to illuminate the space adequately.

Daylight coming from windows, atria, skylights, and clerestories provides full-spectrum light in its purest form. However, if daylight is in short supply, an alternative to bring out the best in a full-spectrum palette is to use full-spectrum fixtures.

Full-spectrum light fixtures, both incandescent and fluorescent, are now available at a reasonable cost. These fixtures come in all sizes, including the 40- and 60-watt incandscent household bulbs. They have a balance of red, blue, and yellow that will enhance any environment.

There is also evidence that some full-spectrum light fixtures do have health benefits. According to a review of the research by designer Millicent Gappell, conventional cool-white fluorescent light at standard indoor levels is interpreted by the human pineal gland as darkness. She also found that studies comparing standard fluorescents and full-spectrum tubes showed that full-spectrum lighting produced significantly less reaction by the stress hormones ACTH and cortisol.

In a two-year study of the nonvisual effects of light on schoolchildren, Warren E. Hathaway, of the Alberta Education Department in Edmonton, Alberta, Canada, found that using ultraviolet-enhanced full-spectrum fluorescent lighting in classrooms made a significant difference in the development of dental cavities, school attendance rates, rates of achievement, and general health and development.

These studies support the notion that a full-spectrum palette, whether produced by light fixtures or the color reflecting off materials and finishes, is beneficial to our health and well-being

ARTWORK FOR COLOR

Art is often selected to enhance the esthetics of interior spaces, but using art is another way to create or refine a full-spectrum palette. Frequently, posters of famous works of art, such as those of the French Impressionist painters Monet, Matisse, and Van Gogh, are selected for their composition and color. However, budget is a major factor and reproductions are often chosen over original works of art.

Nevertheless, since color is energy, the use of original works of art is always preferable. Artists create works of art that have a visionary awareness, style, or signature; and the individual approaches to a full-spectrum color palette are varied. Likewise, original works of art have a life force that reflects the artist's spirit and can lift the viewer's spirits, which also has a positive physiological effect. In 1888, Florence Nightingale wrote, "People say the effect (of art) is only on the mind. It is no such thing. The effect is on the body, too. Little as we know about the way in which we are affected by form, by color and light, we do know this— they have an actual physical effect. Variety of form and brillancy of color in the objects presented to patients are actual means to recovery."

Many artists paint images of current political issues or human suffering. For public spaces (and healthcare facilities in particular), it is recommended that the spiritual content of the work of art be universally harmonious so that anyone can enjoy the artist's intention.

There is little evidence to favor using one type of art over another. In a study of the effect of wall art on patients in a psychiatric ward, Roger Ulrich of Texas A&M University found negative reactions to abstract art. However, it is not clear as to what type of abstract art Ulrich used in this study, only that the content of the art was "ambigu-

ous or completely unclear." It would be a broad assumption to classify all abstract art in this manner and conclude that it produces negative effects. Depending on the subject matter and colors, both abstract and representational art can cause viewers to feel depressed or anxious. Therefore, the spiritual content of the work, color palette, and subject matter, should be carefully considered in choosing art.

The three artists whose works are shown in Figures 2, 3, and 4 are unique in their personal statements, but, at the same time, they each utilize the principles of color theory to create a special harmony that can be used in designing healthy interior spaces. Each artist has a completely different style and subject matter, but all three share the balance and harmony of nature that is so important to a full-spectrum palette.

Diana Kurz paints a still life in a painterly realist style, creating a special harmony in composition with her vivid color choices (Figure 2). Her palette is full-spectrum in that she uses the trinity of red, yellow, and blue in infinite variations of hue, value, and chroma changes. Her deliberate use of the contrast of extension and her silky strokes create an easy path for the eye of the viewer. Kurz is a renowned colorist who always creates a high level of luminosity on canvas.

Joseph DiGiorgio is best known for full-spectrum pointillist landscapes (Figure 3). Using small symmetrical strokes of color in a fluid and continuous pattern, he creates layers of light much like the layers of color seen in nature. He studies the circadian rhythms of light through his travels all over the world. He then features an area and dissects its light changes in value progressions though sketches and photographs. The final work reveals a stong contrast of light and dark that settles the spirit of the viewer by exposure to its familiar sensations of daily natural patterns and rhythms. His use of neutrals throughout his paintings enhances the brighter spots of light.

Laurie Zagon (coauthor of this book) is an abstract colorist. Her work is strongly associated with color theory principles in that she paints a "facsimile" of light on canvas (Figure 4). Her canvases and sculpture reflect the currents and forces at play in nature by focusing on small areas, which are then removed from their original context. The movement of air, as well as the provocative force of a waterlike flow of hues, combined with a tangible three-dimensional element that relates to the physical body versus the spiritual realm, provides a special feeling of colored light and energy. The viewer absorbs the

comfort and security of the recognizable feelings from nature's life force and, therefore, receives a regenerative energy.

DESIGNING A FULL-SPECTRUM COLOR PALETTE

The following is a recommended checklist of planning questions to ask when designing interior spaces with full-spectrum color:

- If remodeling an existing space, what are the existing colors? Which colors must remain? (Keep in mind that permanent hardware and exit signage, for example, have color.) Use this information as a springboard for the color palette.
- What is the desired color temperature of the space? Is it warm (red), cool (blue), or in between (green)? Choose dominant hues accordingly.
- How much natural light is available to enhance the visibility of the color palette?
- What type of other lighting is in use or will be specified? Are incandescent (yellow), halogen (soft yellow), fluorescent (blue), or full-spectrum fluorescent or incandescent lamps to be used?
- Is the palette balanced with representative colors from the major triad of red, yellow, and blue hues? (Remember, brass hardware is yellow based; wood flooring is often yellow or orange based.)
- What accessories, fixtures, furniture, materials, and so forth, are planned for the space? Make a materials and finishes color checklist (see charts in Project Showcase section) and note how much each hue is used.
- Does the materials and finishes checklist show a good balance of all the colors? Does it follow the rules of contrast of extension, as mentioned in Chapter 1 and at the beginning of this chapter?

The next two chapters present a variety of projects that demonstrate good use of full-spectrum color. Since little or no information has been available heretofore on full-spectrum color, most of the designers of these projects planned their color palettes instinctively. Although most designers' instincts about color are good, it stands to reason that more deliberate color planning can only result in better designs that will positively affect the health and well-being of those who will occupy the planned spaces.

4

PROJECT EXAMPLES:

HOSPITALITY, LABORATORIES, OFFICES, SCHOOLS

Using a full-spectrum color palette in an interior space is, in theory, much different than in practice. As mentioned in the preceding chapter, most design professionals create full-spectrum interiors without even knowing it. Yet, to fully harness the power of color to create healthy interiors, a carefully planned color scheme is necessary.

The projects described in this chapter were selected to show the variety of ways in which full-spectrum color can be incorporated. Effective space planning, attention to architectural detail, adequate lighting, and a balanced color palette of materials and finishes all contribute to the "healthfulness" of these interior spaces. Based on the theories discussed in earlier chapters of this book, we can only conclude that this combination of design methods evokes feelings of comfort and cheer that give people a positive sense of health and well-being.

HOSPITALITY

Hotels and restaurants should make people feel comfortable, so as to allow them to relax, rest, or enjoy being entertained. Use of stronger, brighter colors in the spectrum, with greater contrast, provides an uplifting, spirited atmosphere for guests and patrons.

▲
_____

The **Ramada Renaissance Hotel** in New York City is designed with an updated Manhattan Deco style that is lush with subtle, full-spectrum color relationships.

The designers have incorporated a feast of neutralized red, yellow, and blue in the hotel's east salon (Figure 5). Rich espresso-brown fabric, amber and steel-blue-gray marble flooring, and red mahogany and karpa wood cabinetry are set against a pale gray and beige wall mural. Yellow tones are projected by soft yellow halogen lighting and the reflection of the brass trim on furniture and railings.

A typical guest room (Figure 6) features the same luxurious red mahogany cabinetry, along with soft rose and ivory wallcoverings and a pale blue and mauve carpet. Dark pottery and abstract art provide other hues for the palette. The extreme dark and light values give a dramatic look to the room.

28

▲

A spectacular mural enhances the full-spectrum color palette in the trendy theaterlike atmosphere of the **Cypress Club** restaurant in San Francisco, California (Figure 7). Bright, colorful 3-D cartoonlike forms in the mural contrast with opulent red mahogany woods, a pale golden yellow patina on the walls, orange-copper arches, maroon upholstery fabric, and an indigo stone mosaic floor. The warm colors of the spectrum are used in neutral deep, rich low-chroma browns.

Yellow-based halogen lamps keep the light level as soft and flowing as the bulbous curves of the furniture, columns, and railings (Figure 8). This restaurant is a true environmental sculpture, reflecting the designer's background as a painter and sculptor.

LABORATORIES

Traditionally, laboratories have been void of color, resulting from the misguided thinking that neutral gray or tan will not interfere with the concentration of researchers. While use of bright color on large surfaces may prevent accurate observation of materials being tested and analyzed (because of the reflectance factor), the proper balance of full-spectrum color should actually enhance the environment. Use of stronger color on surfaces where visual observation is not so critical, such as furniture and doors, is recommended.

▲

The **Fuller E. Callaway, Jr. Manufacturing Research Center** at Georgia Institute of Technology in Atlanta is an example of a full-spectrum approach to color that can improve the performance of those conducting research in a laboratory facility.

Dedicated to research in manufacturing-related technologies, this 120,000-square-foot building is, in itself, a visual metaphor for engineering systems. Its structure and infrastructure are exposed, while traditional elements of manufacturing—simple machines such as gears, cogs, wheels, conveyor belts, cranes, and hinges—are highlighted in the design.

Full-spectrum color is cleverly integrated on all mechanical systems in the unfinished labs and utility atrium (Figures 9 and 10). According to the designer, these systems are left exposed, color coded, and labeled according to the guidelines of the Occupational Safety and Health Administration (OSHA) to provide awareness, understanding, and ease of maintenance while creating the building esthetic.

Color is specifically used in the utility atrium for economy and accessibility to lab equipment. Specific machinery is identified by the use of high-intensity primary and secondary colors. The total effect is a geometric maze of easily accessible and eye-pleasing color that creates an overall sense of illumination.

Farrohk Mistree, a professor of mechanical engineering at Georgia Tech, finds that the openness of the atrium and its bright colors inspire his laboratory work, and his visions of the future.

The private lab (Figure 11) is purposely outlined in primary red, yellow, and blue and enhanced with split complements of yellow-green and red-violet. The white walls setting off these colorful pipes and machinery give a look of creativity and energy to an interior in which very serious and concentrated work is being done.

OFFICES

The ideal office environment should encourage interaction and support individual work. Unfortunately, many office buildings do not offer all workers good views to the outside, nor do they provide them access to fresh air. With the proper use of full-spectrum color and light, these confined spaces can be transformed to energized, positive work environments. Generally, the rule, again, is to use a balanced palette and avoid large expanses of bright colors. Strong, vibrating colors or extreme light contrasts within the peripheral vision of a person sitting in front of a computer screen are also not recommended.

30

The reception area of the **Apple Learning Center** in Mountain View, California utilizes bold primary colors of red, yellow, and blue to generate a playful spirit for company employees.

Designers effectively used black, white, and gray checkered floors, white walls, and yellow-based natural wood cabinets to balance the full-spectrum palette dominated by the bright colors (Figure 12).

In **Burger King's Corporate World Headquarters** in Miami, Florida, the colors and textures of a hamburger provided inspiration for the carpet design (Figure 13), from which a full-spectrum palette emerges. Used in large-scale abstract patterns, color creates a transparent illusion of various geometric shapes that appear to be swimming on the floor. White walls and system furniture, though maybe not the best choice for work areas (because of glare and high reflectance values), allow the carpet color to be visually dominant in corridors and open spaces.

By using a full-spectrum color palette and natural motifs, designers imparted a personal feeling to the office areas of the patent law firm of **Marshall O'Toole Gerstein Murray & Borun** in Chicago. Cleverly introduced through a combination of earth tones and amorphic shapes (Figures 14 and 15), the colors and patterns are inspired by autumn images. Natural cherry, raisin, amber, and doeskin hues interact and harmonize with moss, forest, and slate-green hues, creating a complementary color harmony. Abstractions of foliage (bark and water) and patinated metals echo in the carpet, glass, wallcoverings, and upholstery.

The use of patterned translucent glass in doors and walls welcomes natural light into interior spaces and provides added visual interest by creating engaging light patterns suggestive of light passing through leaves. Artwork in the conference room and corridors further enhances the full-spectrum palette.

▲

The traditional design of **Price Waterhouse** in New York City incorporates a simple red, yellow, and blue full-spectrum color palette. In the reception area (Figure 16) designers offset the red-based mahogany woodwork with a marble floor of eggshell colored rectangular stripes on a bluish-black, veinlike pattern. Incandescent (yellow) lamps and fluorescent (blue) fixtures complete this triad of primaries.

Woodwork dominates the rather conservative office areas (Figure 17), which are balanced by a dusty blue carpet, coordinating fabric, and colorful artwork.

▲

The designers of **Simon Marketing's** office in Oak Brook Terrace, Illinois, created a full-spectrum palette by using multiple variations of the primary and secondary hues. In the conference room, a red-orange panel dominates (Figure 18) because of its size. This color is juxtaposed nicely with an abstract work of art on the wall, which features yellow, yellow-orange, and dark blue-green. Whether intentional or not, the conference table surface reflects the powerful colors of the room. Charcoal gray carpet and an undulating silver corrugated wall supply the neutral tones needed to create the jewellike harmony of the pure hues.

Private offices (Figure 19) feature pastel walls of pink with a middle value of blue-violet painted on inside of openings. Soft yellow halogen lighting repeats the trio of red, yellow, and blue set against a deep charcoal carpet.

32

SCHOOLS

A school should be a fun place that encourages learning. Again, the use of full-spectrum color creates an energy that is uplifting and positive. Children love color and respond to it well—but that does not mean the only approach is to use primaries. Use of high-reflectance colors in corridors and stairways, and sharp accent colors on railings and doors, can define points of orientation. In the classroom, the color palette should not be a distraction; rather, it should promote concentration through use of a neutral palette with accent brights.

▲

The designers' eclectic use of materials and finishes gives **Cesar Chavez Elementary School** in Chicago a robust full-spectrum palette. This 55,000-square-foot facility was built for the Chicago Public School system to serve 550 children from kindergarten to eighth grade. Located on a less than half-acre site, it shares a city block with other commercial buildings.

Color is effectively used to create a special identity that distinguishes the school against the gray and brown backdrop of the city. Full-spectrum color is clearly defined on both the exterior and interior through the consistent usage of geometric patterns and shapes.

An exterior photo (Figure 20) shows bricks of five different colors inlaid with geometric patterns that are in the red, blue, and yellow families set against the natural elements of color—blue sky and green grass. Accents of bright yellow and red are also used on the facade to complete the full-spectrum palette.

The entry vestibule (Figure 21) repeats the bright yellow and red in large geometric sections painted with gloss enamels. The floor is a light neutral blue gray with a pattern of one-foot squares in blue, yellow, red, and white, which repeat the natural flow of this geometric harmony. Walls are painted in yellow-gray, blue-gray, and sky blue.

Daylight coming in through the skylights adds to the full-spectrum look of the project by providing more illumination for visibility. Incandescent light allows a warmer, yellower light to be projected against the often dominant cool blue tones.

An otherwise gray corridor (Figure 22) is enlivened through the use of colored "light boxes" recessed into the walls. The distinct forms, colors, and textures used in this project make it a school building that is as intriguing, exciting, and delightful as learning.

▲

Taking advantage of the red rocks of Sedona, Arizona, as a backdrop, the designers of **Big Park Elementary School** in the Village of Oak Creek, used a natural palette of red-oranges, red-violets, violets, and blue-greens to reinforce the colors of this scenic environment (Figure 23). The building exterior softly reiterates the tones of the red rocks, while the surrounding landscaping creates a glorious use of red-green complementary harmony.

The school's interior walls are painted in a high-gloss off-white, creating warmth as well as a netural background. The carpet used throughout is composed of full-spectrum colors, ranging from a middle-chroma red-orange to blue-green, red-violet, and blue-violet. Cabinets and furniture in variations of blue-green, red-orange, and yellow cream also accent the interior (Figure 24). In addition, designers used color to designate various grade levels and to aid in wayfinding. Most of the windows in the building face the inspiring vistas of the rocks.

▲

For the **Patwin Elementary School** in Davis, California designers used a full-spectrum palette of pastel blue, green, red, and yellow on the building exterior (which, because of the mild California climate, can also be thought of as the school's interior). Students spend a great amount of their school day in common areas outdoors between classes, eating, exercising, and playing. Multiple surfaces of color facilitate the energy of these activities throughout the school grounds (Figure 25).

5

PROJECT
EXAMPLES:
HEALTHCARE

Healthcare environments constitute a specialized area of design. Here the proper use of color can play an important role in healing, which is both a physical and a mental process. Research into mind/body medicine has indicated that the less stress patients feel, the more likely they are to recover quickly from an illness. Anxiety over treatment, unfamiliarity with the treatment delivery process, and the very nature of the clinical environment all contribute to stress.

Historically, clinical environments have been sterile, shiny, clean—and therefore cold and foreboding. The current approach is to "soften" the healthcare environment and make it more welcoming and warm. Using a full-spectrum color palette is one way of achieving this goal.

A few recommended "dos and don'ts" in designing healthcare environments are as follows:

- A balanced color palette will eliminate problems associated with using too much yellow (which tends to make patients look jaundiced).
- Using the opposite color of red (green) as the dominant color in operating rooms may lessen eyestrain for surgeons as they move the focus of their eyes from body tissue to the surrounding environment.
- Hues of similar saturation and value should not be placed side by side in facilities for the elderly. The reason is that as people age, the lens of the eye turns yellow-brown, and hues of similar saturation and value next to each other become blurred, thus making it difficult to interpret environmental information (such as depth, contrast of objects, etc.).

Although dark red, red-orange, and red-violet have been found to be among the most easily visible and discernible colors for elderly people (especially when juxtaposed with white or near white), these colors should be used only in balance with the rest of the full-spectrum palette. Careful selection of colors can help increase contrast sensitivity and eliminate glare, both of which are important to the aging or impaired eye.

To provide optimum contrast for people with low vision, the authors of a technical guide to selecting colors for partially sighted people, published by The Lighthouse Research Institute in New York City, advise the following:

- Maximize intensity/reflectance contrast.
- Contrast dark colors with the opposite extremes of the hue scale, with tints from mid-value scale colors, and avoid contrasting light

colors from the extremes of the hue scale against dark mid-value scale colors.

- Avoid the use of any color against an achromatic color (white, gray, black) of similar value.
- Avoid contrasting hues from adjacent parts of the hue scale.
- Avoid constrasting colors of low chroma and similar value.

AMBULATORY/OUTPATIENT CARE CENTERS

▲

A contemporary Mexican architectural style was selected by the designers of the **Ambulatory Surgical Center/Scripps Memorial Hospital** in Encinitas, California, to introduce colorful original folk art, and because the community has a great affinity for things Mexican. This project's lively full-spectrum color palette is uplifting and energizing for patients awaiting or undergoing surgery.

Pastel tones of blue-violet, red, and teal, as well as the natural yellow wood tones of the cabinets, pale peach walls, and oatmeal ceilings create a festive backdrop for the folk art objects placed throughout the waiting area (Figures 26-27). Dominant off-white tones harmonize with colorful full-spectrum accents on windows, cabinets, and partitions. The result is a healthy balance of each hue that is soothing and calming.

▲

Designers for the **Cancer Center at St. Francis Hospital and Medical Center** in Hartford, Connecticut, used full-spectrum color in a most subtle way. Because the first-floor reception area (Figure 28) is circular in plan, they designed the floor as a series of circles extending from a common tangency. Each circle is noted by its color change in warm and cool greenish-grays.

The natural yellow-based wood cabinetry and furniture are complemented by the cool, deep solid blue-green tones and the deep red-mauve and blue-green floral print upholstery fabric. Floor-to-ceiling windows permit a steady flood of outside light.

A soft watercolor-like effect of full-spectrum color accents a private treatment room (Figure 29), which has a large window that provides a view of outside gardens. The blue-violet-gray and rose-gray floral fabric on the chairs and a yellow leather recliner are set beautifully against the yellow-orange-tinted peach walls. A pale peach tone is used in a geometric pattern on the floor with a deep indigo that creates a grayed palette of full-spectrum color.

DAY CARE

▲

Mattel Child Development Center in Los Angeles, features a colorful full-spectrum entryway that is a welcome change from outside to in. The designers painted the corridor walls in a bright sunshine yellow that is appropriate for this type of space, particularly when used in its highest intensity. These yellow walls are juxtaposed with intense primary color stripes of red, orange, blue, and green, which are designed to create a cool-to-warmer mood change from the reception area to the office spaces (Figure 30).

In the play area (Figure 31), blue-green and yellow-green pie-cut-shaped ceiling sections balance the amorphic shape of the sea-blue carpet on the floor, which is set in a gray-green background. Accents of the primaries scattered throughout the project create a fun feeling without an overdose of intense color, which has been known to cause hyperactivity in children.

HOSPITALS

▲
_____

Children's Hospital and Health Center, Patient Care Pavilion in San Diego, California, was designed to meet the special needs of children while reflecting the character of its southwestern locale. To inspire the imagination of children, the designers playfully incorporated a full-spectrum of bright, cheerful colors and unusual combinations of shapes and sizes.

The exterior walls of the upper floor are finished in a cream-colored stucco, juxtaposed at the base with a darker material of alternating masonry textures (Figure 32). The interior color palette is balanced by salmon and yellow walls and a light-blue ceiling.

Furniture and carpeting in the waiting area (Figure 33) show a full-spectrum array of complementary colors. Patient rooms (Figure 34) are painted with pale ice cream hues in pink, yellow, green, orange, and blue. Built-in cabinetry in the rooms and nurses' station are highlighted with bold Matisse-like variations of the wall and ceiling colors.

_____

▲
_____

HealthPark Medical Center in Fort Meyers, Florida, incorporates full-spectrum color in its lobby with unusual lighting, to achieve a wonderful dreamlike setting (see sidebar, page 40). This space is interesting because it represents the cutting edge in the use of full-spectrum color to promote healing and closely parallels a hospitality environment.

There is an automatic sense of splendor upon arrival at this hospital. An arrangement of high intensity blue, green, violet, red, orange, and yellow lamps wash the lobby walls with rainbows of color (Figure 35). When asked about his work with colored light in hospitals, Craig Roeder, the lighting designer for the project, told *Architectural Record Lighting,* "It's a hospital. People walk into it worried and sick. I tried to design an entrance space that provides them with light and energy—to 'beam them up' a little bit before they get to the patient rooms."

To enliven a long corridor that connects two of the most important buildings at the **Mayo Clinic** in Rochester, Minnesota, designers created a spectacular color relief mural (Figure 36). On the left, shades and tints of red are used in orderly proportions to create a third dimension, as well as a visual wayfinding effect down this lengthy corridor. The rightside of the walkway is identical in form, but changes in hue to a range of low-chroma blues that repeat the same orderly system of the red side. Soft and warm yellowish lighting completes the triad of red, yellow, and blue. When the triad of colors are present in a space, an immediate harmony is created. Gray carpeting acts as a neutral force, holding both sides together and enhancing the hues to make them clearer and brighter.

The color palette in **Vidarkliniken,** a healing center in an anthroposophical community in Jarna, Sweden, was derived from Rudolph Steiner's work on color. Steiner described color as a "living experience" and focused on environmental color brought indoors. As mentioned in Chapter 3, Vidarkliniken is one of the few healthcare facilities that use color as part of the healing experience.

Corridors (Figure 37) are painted in a warm yellow and feature natural wood floors. A pink room with green chairs (Figure 38) is utilized as a meditation or counseling room. Using the lazur method of painting, the designer applied frescolike, thin coats of rich transparent color on the walls, layer by layer, to reach a specific level of luminosity. The use of warm and cool strongly reflects Steiner's philosophy that color should always reinforce the function of a space.

The luminosity created by the color appears to be *in* the walls, rather than *on* the walls. The eye is able to rest from the pink walls by seeing green on the chairs, and the landscape outside creates a complementary realtionship. Yellow lighting adds further warmth so that the color temperature of the room is dominantly warm, with cool spots to rest the eye.

arrived in Ft. Meyers on a Friday night and worked with the electricians 'till the wee hours of the morning putting color here and there. I was attempting to psychically channel the creative energies of abstract expressionist painter Jackson Pollock, but the light looked terrible. And worse, I still didn't know what to do.

I had all these wonderful colors, but I couldn't make them make sense. The space looked like something from a third-grade finger painting class. Finally, Scarlett O'Hara visited to remind me, "After all, tomorrow is another day."

I later lay in bed planning my day, beginning with a couple of hours of fun swimming at the beach. Instead, it was pouring rain, totally overcast, and a miserable day. So I made myself a pot of coffee and sat on the lanai outside my room overlooking the bay. There I meditated. (When God gives you lemons, make lemonade.) I remembered a time in Mescalero, N.M., when I had a little luck in getting the clouds to separate so I could see the sun. I thought, "God, what am I going to do about all these colors that these nice people have spent all this money on?"

Just as I opened my eyes, the sky opened up and, dear Gussy, a huge rainbow came plunging into the day. As if that weren't enough, at the same moment, a school of porpoises swam into the bay. During the years I worked in Hawaii, the Kahonas of Manelli Bay told me that if the wild porpoises allow you to swim with them, you are filled with spiritual energy. And they always swim with me.

As I saw the porpoises swimming in the bay—the only time I have ever seem porpoises in Ft. Myers—tears flowed down my cheeks. I realized I was having a full-blown, gala-induced, spiritual experience—an illumination epiphany, if you will.

41

"I get it; rainbows of light. Sounds like a prizewinner to me. Thank you, Father," I prayed. It pays to stay in touch with your higher power.

The ceiling lights in the atrium are on an astronomical time clock. The lamps are on about three-six hours a day, depending on the time of year. In addition, metal halide uplights underneath the palms work as a very nice night-lite circuit. The lamps that run all night are on the ground and easier to change. Cold cathode cover lighting (3000 K) surrounds the atrium opening. Total energy consumption in the atrium is 0.9 W/ft^2, thanks to new energy-saving sources.

Corridors

The vision for corridor lighting came from my childhood when my adenoids and tonsils were removed. I was given an injection to make me groggy. The operating room wasn't ready so I was left on my gurney out in the hall. All the time I was staring into horrible two by four foot fluorescent lights. It was worse than anything I experienced during the 1970s.

That experience motivated me to remember HealthPark's patients. Energy efficiency was important, but I wanted each patient to have as pleasant experience as possible. It was not easy to convince the hospital to take this approach. Instead, they questioned my involvement with the project. But after hearing my story, Mary Wright of Medical Space Design supported me, as did [Noel] Barrick [the project architect]. So we got it done.

—Excerpted from "High, Higher, Highest: Spiritual Reveries Inspire Lighting Design" by Craig A. Roeder (*Lighting Design and Application*, March 1993).

LONG-TERM CARE

▲

Light and dark hues make up the full-spectrum palette for the **Casa Palmera Care Center** in Del Mar, California. For the living room, which overlooks an outdoor courtyard (Figure 39), the designers used large proportions of mauve and slate-blue on walls and floors, which contrast with the colors in the sofa upholstery and architectural elements. Accessories and artwork complete the full-spectrum palette in this space.

Rose-colored tile flooring in a corridor outside resident rooms (Figure 40) is color balanced with a pink, orange, yellow, and blue-green tile water fountain.

▲

For the library at **Karrington on the Scioto,** a 53-unit assisted living facility in Columbus, Ohio, designers used a rich full-spectrum palette in contrasting hues and shades to create a friendly environment for the aging eye (Figure 43). A tapestry of blue, red, violet, and tan fabric adorns a large sofa, which is flanked by two bright red chairs. Other upholstered chairs feature blue-green, green, blue, red, and tan colors. Red fabric is draped at windows, which are outlined in white for easy detection. An oak floor, brass fixtures, and accessories add yellow to the palette. Walls above the chair rail are covered in a light-blue paper; the lower walls, painted a darker blue, rest on a white baseboard to contrast with the oak floor. Crown molding in a darker blue than the wallcovering outlines the ceiling.

MEDICAL OFFICES

▲

Designers created a warm, hearthlike feeling for the office of the **Department of Cardiothoracic Surgery at Columbia**

Presbyterian Medical Center in New York City by using warm red- and yellow-orange-based wood for the floor, as well as for cabinets, doors, and trim.

An original painting of New England fall foliage connects a private office (Figure 41) with the energy of the outdoors. The painting, along with a blue stone slate desk, gray-blue upholstery, red- and yellow-orange wood, and green plants, establishes a beautiful harmony of full-spectrum color.

In the waiting room (Figure 42), an almost Japanese-like simplicity is carried through with a yellow-orange wood floor, original art, and warm gray sofas placed opposite a contemporary red-orange chair. The lighting is soft white-yellow halogen, and the room is accented with a tall green plant in one corner. The two works of art are powerful images and provide detail to this very sparse, but elegant, space.

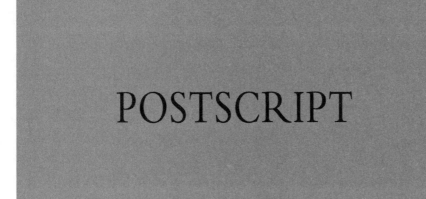

POSTSCRIPT

What is necessary for full-spectrum color to become part of the design professional's vocabulary of skills? Those involved in color selection need to:

- Shift the focus of color in interior design away from trends and toward methodology.
- Educate clients about full-spectrum color and its potential healthful effects.
- Document projects in which they consciously use full-spectrum color.
- Conduct or sponsor research that demonstrates the health effects of a full-spectrum color palette on those who use a space so designed, and make the results of these studies available to everyone in the profession.

For too many years, color has been underrated in the field of architecture and interior design. Its value in promoting good health becomes more apparent every day in its comforting and mood-altering abilities. Color is literally the "wavelength" medicine of the future. It calls to us and asks us to recognize its value as an alternative medicine that the environment can provide.

Why are organizations and individuals not investing in the research required to create data supporting the physiologically healthy effects of color? We have in the United States, the finest scholars and scientists in the specialty fields of biology, engineering, physics, and so forth, to contribute to a consortium of research that would validate color's role in human health. A worldwide nonprofit color research center could be established, whose function would be to fund studies on the healthy

properties of color energy in all its forms. This information could be accessible to anyone and utilized via a master database that publishes and distributes its findings.

True visionaries can see how things can be instead of how things are. We need to become color visionaries as we contemplate the future of design for healthy interior spaces. We need to collaborate with each other, as in the Bauhaus School of Design in the 1940s, when Gropius, Itten, Kandinsky, Albers, and others envisioned color theory education in design schools. Let us focus less on the marketing of color and be less motivated by financial gain. Instead, we should be more motivated by the service we can give to our communities through the results of research on the health-enhancing effects of color. By so doing, we will realize a kind in prosperity of working with color beyond our wildest dreams.

PROJECT SHOWCASE

COLOR WHEEL

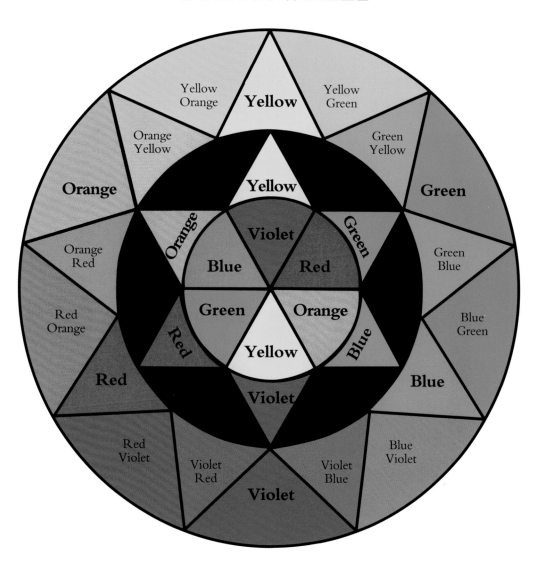

FIGURE 1

When the primary colors of red, yellow, and blue and the secondary colors of orange, green, and violet are arranged in a consecutive circular order, a continuous flow of harmony is apparent.

FIGURE 2

Artwork: *3 Pears and a Lemon. Oil on canvas.*
Artist: *Diana Kurz, New York, N.Y.*
Photographer: *Kevin Noble.*

FIGURE 3
Artwork: *Hudson River Series. Oil on canvas.*
Artist: *Joseph DiGiorgio, New York, N.Y.*
Photographer: *Leda Moser.*

FIGURE 4
Artwork: *Speed of Light. Oil on canvas.*
Artist: *Laurie Zagon, Flagstaff, Ariz.*
Photographer: *Jim Koch.*

FIGURES 5 & 6
Project: *Ramada Renaissance Hotel.*
Location: *New York, N.Y.*
Design: *DiLeonardo International.*
Photography: *Tom Crane.*

Ramada Renaissance Hotel

Materials & Finishes	R	O	Y	G	B	V
Artwork	•	•	•	•	•	•
Accessories			•			•
Ceilings			•			•
Floors	•		•		•	•
Furniture/Cabinetry	•	•				
Hardware			•		•	
Lighting			•			
Plants				•		
Upholstery	•	•			•	•
Walls & Wallcoverings	•	•	•			•
Windowcoverings						
Woodwork	•	•				

Most Important Contrasts: *Light and Dark, Cold and Warm,
Extension*

Cypress Club

Materials & Finishes	R	O	Y	G	B	V
Artwork	•	•	•	•	•	•
Accessories	•					
Ceilings			•			•
Floors	•	•				
Furniture/Cabinetry	•	•			•	
Hardware		•				
Lighting			•			
Plants				•		
Upholstery	•					
Walls & Wallcoverings	•		•			
Windowcoverings						
Woodwork	•					

Most Important Contrasts: *Cold and Warm, Complements, Extension*

FIGURES 7 & 8
Project: *Cypress Club.*
Location: *San Francisco, Calif.*
Design: *Jordan Mozer & Associates.*
Photography: *Dennis Anderson.*

FIGURES 9, 10, 11
Project: *Fuller E. Callaway, Jr., Manufacturing Research Center, Georgia Institute of Technology.*
Location: *Atlanta, Ga.*
Design: *Lord Aeck & Sargent.*
Photography: *Jonathan Hillyer Photography.*

Fuller E. Callaway, Jr., Manufacturing Research Center

Materials & Finishes	R	O	Y	G	B	V
Artwork						
Accessories						
Ceilings						
Floors					•	
Furniture/Cabinetry						
Hardware	•	•	•	•	•	•
Lighting			•		•	
Plants						
Upholstery	•	•				
Walls & Wallcoverings						
Windowcoverings						
Woodwork						
Most Important Contrasts: *Hue, Saturation*						

Apple Learning Center

Materials & Finishes	R	O	Y	G	B	V
Artwork						
Accessories						
Ceilings						
Floors	•		•		•	•
Furniture/Cabinetry	•		•		•	
Hardware					•	
Lighting			•		•	
Plants						
Upholstery	•		•		•	
Walls & Wallcoverings						
Windowcoverings						
Woodwork		•	•			

Most Important Contrasts: *Hue, Light and Dark, Extension*

FIGURE 12

Project: *Apple Learning Center.*
Location: *Mountain View, Calif.*
Design: *STUDIOS Architecture.*
Photography: *Sharon Risedorph.*

Burger King
Corporate World Headquarters

Materials & Finishes	R	O	Y	G	B	V
Artwork						
Accessories						
Ceilings						
Floors	•	•	•	•	•	•
Furniture/Cabinetry			•			
Hardware						
Lighting			•		•	
Plants						
Upholstery	•	•	•	•	•	•
Walls & Wallcoverings						
Windowcoverings						
Woodwork						

Most Important Contrasts: *Hue, Saturation*

FIGURE 13

Project: *Burger King Headquarters.*
Location: *Miami, Fla.*
Design: *NBBJ.*
Photography: *Paul Warchol.*

Marshall O'Toole Gerstein Murray & Borun

Materials & Finishes	R	O	Y	G	B	V
Artwork	•	•	•	•	•	•
Accessories	•	•			•	
Ceilings			•	•		
Floors	•	•	•	•		
Furniture/Cabinetry	•	•				
Hardware				•		
Lighting				•		
Plants	•			•		
Upholstery	•	•	•	•	•	•
Walls & Wallcoverings				•	•	•
Windowcoverings						
Woodwork	•	•	•			

Most Important Contrasts: *Hue, Saturation, Extension*

FIGURES 14 & 15
Project: *Marshall O'Toole Gerstein Murray & Borun.*
Location: *Chicago, Ill.*
Design: *Mekus Johnson.*
Photography: *Jon Miller, Hedrich-Blessing.*

Price Waterhouse

Materials & Finishes	R	O	Y	G	B	V
Artwork					•	
Accessories				•		
Ceilings				•		
Floors				•	•	•
Furniture/Cabinetry	•	•				
Hardware				•	•	
Lighting				•	•	
Plants						
Upholstery				•	•	•
Walls & Wallcoverings				•		
Windowcoverings						
Woodwork		•				

Most Important Contrasts: *Hue, Light and Dark, Saturation*

FIGURES 16 & 17
Project: *Price Waterhouse.*
Location: *New York, N.Y.*
Design: *ISI.*
Photography: *Marco Lorenzetti, Hedrich-Blessing.*

Simon Marketing

Materials & Finishes	R	O	Y	G	B	V
Artwork		•	•	•	•	•
Accessories	•	•			•	•
Ceilings						
Floors					•	
Furniture/Cabinetry					•	
Hardware					•	
Lighting				•	•	
Plants						
Upholstery					•	
Walls & Wallcoverings	•	•			•	
Windowcoverings						
Woodwork						

Most Important Contrasts: *Hue, Light and Dark, Extension*

FIGURES 18 & 19
Project: Simon Marketing.
Location: Oak Brook Terrace, Ill.
Design: Griswold, Heckel, & Kelly.
Photography: Wayne Cable.

FIGURES 20, 21, 22
Project: *Cesar Chavez Elementary School.*
Location: *Chicago, Ill.*
Design: *Ross Barney + Jankowski Inc.*
Photography: *Steve Hall, Hedrich-Blessing.*

Cesar Chavez Elementary School

Materials & Finishes	R	O	Y	G	B	V
Artwork						
Accessories		•				
Ceilings	•	•			•	
Floors	•		•	•	•	•
Furniture/Cabinetry						
Hardware					•	
Lighting			•		•	
Plants						
Upholstery			•	•	•	
Walls & Wallcoverings	•	•	•		•	
Windowcoverings						
Woodwork						

Most Important Contrasts: *Hue, Saturation*

Big Park Elementary School

Materials & Finishes	R	O	Y	G	B	V
Artwork						
Accessories						
Ceilings			•			
Floors	•	•	•	•	•	•
Furniture/Cabinetry	•	•		•	•	
Hardware					•	
Lighting			•		•	
Plants	•	•		•		
Upholstery						
Walls & Wallcoverings			•			
Windowcoverings						
Woodwork						

Most Important Contrasts: *Hue, Cold and Warm, Complements, Extension*

FIGURES 23, 24
Project: *Big Park Elementary School.*
Location: *Village of Oak Creek, Ariz.*
Design: *Lescher and Mahoney, Inc. / DLR Group.*
Photography: *Dave Tate.*

FIGURE 25

Project: *Patwin Elementary School.*
Location: *Davis, Calif.*
Design: *The Steinberg Group, Architects.*
Photography: *Chas McGrath.*

Patwin Elementary School

Materials & Finishes	R	O	Y	G	B	V
Artwork						
Accessories						
Ceilings						
Floors						
Furniture/Cabinetry						
Hardware					•	
Lighting						
Plants				•		
Upholstery						
Walls & Wallcoverings	•	•	•	•	•	•
Windowcoverings						
Woodwork						

Most Important Contrasts: *Hue, Complements*

FIGURES 26 & 27
Project: *Ambulatory Surgical Center/Scripps Memorial Hospital.*
Location: *Encinitas, Calif.*
Design: *Jain Malkin, Inc.*
Photography: *Steve McClelland.*

Ambulatory Surgical Center/Scripps

Materials & Finishes	R	O	Y	G	B	V
Artwork	•	•	•	•	•	•
Accessories	•	•	•	•	•	•
Ceilings						
Floors			•	•		
Furniture/Cabinetry			•			
Hardware			•			
Lighting			•			
Plants				•		
Upholstery				•	•	•
Walls & Wallcoverings	•	•		•	•	
Windowcoverings						
Woodwork			•			

Most Important Contrasts: *Hue, Light and Dark, Cold and Warm, Saturation, Extension*

Cancer Center at St. Francis Hospital

Materials & Finishes	R	O	Y	G	B	V
Artwork						
Accessories						
Ceilings					•	
Floors			•		•	
Furniture/Cabinetry			•		•	
Hardware					•	
Lighting			•		•	
Plants				•		
Upholstery	•		•	•	•	•
Walls & Wallcoverings			•			
Windowcoverings						
Woodwork		•	•			

Most Important Contrasts: *Light and Dark, Complements*

FIGURES 28 & 29

Project: *Cancer Center, St. Francis Hospital & Medical Center.*
Location: *Hartford, Conn.*
Design: *TRO/The Ritchie Organization.*
Photography: *Warren Jagger.*

Mattel Child Development Center

Materials & Finishes	R	O	Y	G	B	V
Artwork						
Accessories	•		•	•	•	
Ceilings			•	•	•	
Floors			•	•	•	
Furniture/Cabinetry						
Hardware					•	
Lighting			•		•	
Plants						
Upholstery			•	•	•	•
Walls & Wallcoverings	•		•		•	
Windowcoverings						
Woodwork			•			

Most Important Contrasts: *Hue, Extension*

FIGURES 30 & 31
Project: *Mattel Child Development Center.*
Location*: Los Angeles, Calif.*
Design: *David Rios & Associates.*
Photography: *David Hewitt/Anne Garrison.*

FIGURES 32, 33, 34
Project: *Children's Hospital and Health Center, Patient Care Pavilion.*
Location: *San Diego, Calif.*
Design: *NBBJ.*
Photography: *David Hewitt/Anne Garrison.*

Children's Hospital and Health Center

Materials & Finishes	R	O	Y	G	B	V
Artwork	•	•	•	•	•	•
Accessories	•	•	•		•	•
Ceilings			•		•	
Floors	•	•	•	•	•	
Furniture/Cabinetry	•		•		•	•
Hardware			•		•	
Lighting			•		•	
Plants						
Upholstery	•	•			•	•	•
Walls & Wallcoverings	•	•	•			
Windowcoverings						
Woodwork						

Most Important Contrasts: *Hue, Saturation, Extension*

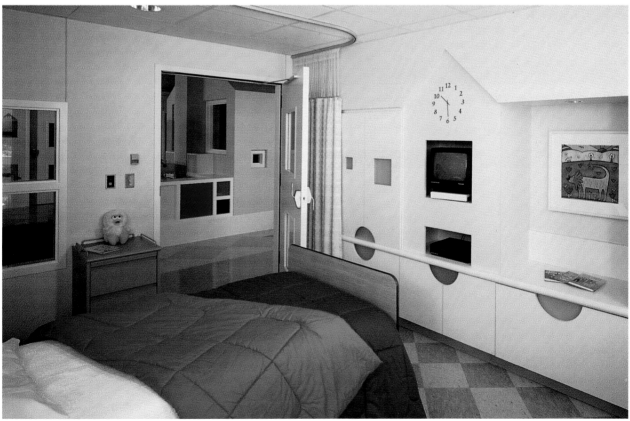

Health Park Medical Center

Materials & Finishes	R	O	Y	G	B	V
Artwork						
Accessories						
Ceilings						
Floors	•		•		•	•
Furniture/Cabinetry						
Hardware			•		•	
Lighting	•	•	•	•	•	•
Plants				•		
Upholstery						
Walls & Wallcoverings						
Windowcoverings						
Woodwork						
Most Important Contrasts: *Hue*						

FIGURE 35

Project: *Health Park Medical Center.*
Location: *Fort Myers, Fla.*
Interior Design/Architecture: *HKS Inc. Architects.*
Lighting Design: *Craig A. Roeder and Associates.*
Photography: *Robt. Ames Cook.*

Mayo Clinic

Materials & Finishes	R	O	Y	G	B	V
Artwork	•				•	•
Accessories						
Ceilings						
Floors					•	
Furniture/Cabinetry						
Hardware		•				
Lighting					•	
Plants						
Upholstery						
Walls & Wallcoverings			•			
Windowcoverings						
Woodwork						

Most Important Contrasts: *Hue, Simultaneity*

FIGURE 36

Project: *Mayo Clinic.*
Location: *Rochester, Minn.*
Design: *Ellerbe Becket.*
Photography: *Peter Aaron/ESTO.*

FIGURES 37 & 38
Project: *Vidarkliniken Healing Center.*
Location: *Jarna, Sweden.*
Design: *Erik Asmussen.*
Photography: *Max Plunger.*

Vidarkliniken Healing Center

Materials & Finishes	R	O	Y	G	B	V
Artwork						
Accessories						•
Ceilings					•	
Floors		•	•		•	
Furniture/Cabinetry	•					
Hardware			•		•	
Lighting			•			
Plants						
Upholstery						
Walls & Wallcoverings	•		•	•		
Windowcoverings						
Woodwork			•			

Most Important Contrasts: *Complements, Saturation*

FIGURES 39 & 40
Project: *Casa Palmera Care Center.*
Location: *Del Mar, Calif.*
Interior Design: *Suzi King Interior Design.*
Architecture: *Galvin Cristilli Architects.*
Photography: *Dennis Mock Photography.*

Casa Palmera

Materials & Finishes	R	O	Y	G	B	V
Artwork	•	•	•		•	•
Accessories	•		•		•	•
Ceilings						
Floors	•				•	
Furniture/Cabinetry			•	•		
Hardware						
Lighting			•			
Plants				•		
Upholstery	•			•	•	
Walls & Wallcoverings	•					
Windowcoverings						
Woodwork			•			

Most Important Contrasts: *Light and Dark, Cold and Warm, Extension*

Dept. of Cardiothoracic Surgery/ Columbia Presbyterian

Materials & Finishes	R	O	Y	G	B	V
Artwork	•	•	•	•	•	•
Accessories				•		
Ceilings						
Floors	•	•	•			
Furniture/Cabinetry					•	•
Hardware						
Lighting				•		
Plants				•		
Upholstery		•	•			
Walls & Wallcoverings						
Windowcoverings						
Woodwork	•	•	•			

Most Important Contrasts: *Light and Dark, Cold and Warm*

FIGURES 41 & 42
Project: *Cardiothoracic Surgery Office,*
Columbia Presbyterian Medical Center.
Location: *New York, N.Y.*
Design: *Pasanella + Klein Stolzman + Berg.*
Photography: *Chuck Choi.*

Karrington on the Scioto

Materials & Finishes	R	O	Y	G	B	V
Artwork			•	•		
Accessories	•		•			
Ceilings						
Floors			•		•	
Furniture/Cabinetry	•					
Hardware			•			
Lighting			•			
Plants				•		
Upholstery	•	•		•	•	•
Walls & Wallcoverings				•		
Windowcoverings	•					
Woodwork				•		

Most Important Contrasts: *Hue, Light and Dark, Cold and Warm, Extension*

FIGURE 43

Project: *Karrington on the Scioto.*
Location: *Columbus, Ohio.*
Design: *Martha Child Interiors.*
Photography: *Skip Meachen.*

Appendix:
THE DESIGN
OF HEALING
ENVIRONMENTS

Authors' Note:

Color is only one design component of a healthy interior space. In recent years, the term healing environment *has been widely used, but perhaps not well understood. What really constitutes an environment that promotes healing and supports well-being? The following excerpt is from a paper written by Jain Malkin based on a talk she gave at the Sixth Symposium on Healthcare Design, which was published in the* Journal of Healthcare Design, Volume VI *(The Center for Health Design, 1994). Although the article focuses on healthcare environments, we think it is appropriate to include as an appendix to this book, because it offers a good explanation of what a healing environment is—information we think can, and should be, applied to all types of interior spaces.*

There is considerable confusion about what constitutes a healing environment. Many recent articles use this term in referring to what we have come to know as the "hospitality healthcare design" trend of the 1980s. While some hotels have a high level of design and drama, which may be esthetically appealing, they generally lack those qualities that might be considered restorative or conducive to physical, emotional, and spiritual healing.

Similarly, many art programs are called "art for healing." However, more often than not, the selection of images has not been based on the scientific research that should form the basis for these selections. Textile art (woven tapestries, patchwork quilts) may be comforting to some individuals and remind them of home and hearth, but scientific literature does not support the idea that because these are textured and created of yarn or cloth, they are "healing."

The criterion should be that appropriate art images actually elicit specific physiological responses that can be predicted. A corollary is that wrong types of images can actually cause stress and stimulate the release of stress hormones into the blood.

The word "healing" is derived from the Anglo-Saxon word *haelen,* and means to be or become whole. Wholeness, or harmony of mind-body-spirit, is a dynamic process of balance at all levels, from the cellular, biological level through the transpersonal and spiritual levels. All the environmental and clinical issues that contribute to a healing or restorative environment are focused toward facilitating patients' movement toward wholeness—toward balance. This goal may be accomplished along with the curing of disease or in the absence of such curing. A person may have a terminal illness, yet may leave the hospital feeling at peace; he or she still has the illness, but the fear and despair are gone. This person is now empowered to examine his or her life with new insight.

In fact, there is an organization in northern California called "Commonweal" that offers retreats for cancer patients (many of whom are terminally ill), to help them heal. In this regard, it should be noted that The Institute of Noetic Sciences recently published a research report documenting close to 4,000 cases worldwide of spontaneous remission. Spontaneous remission is often defined as self-repair. It is fascinating to read case histories of people who had been told they had two to six months to live who then—through deep personal analysis of their life-styles, attitudes, and reactions to stress—were able to stimulate their immune systems to fight the cancer, forcing it into remission.

So, to achieve balance or wholeness for patients, we must appreciate the relationship between mind, body, and spirit, which we might think of as a new trinity.

ASSUMPTIONS UNDERLYING MIND/BODY RESEARCH

There are a number of assumptions that underlie mind/body research and form a common thread among most non-allopathic systems of medicine such as those practiced in China and India.

- According to Janet Quinn, Ph.D., RN, people *are* energy fields—physicists tell us this is true—it's not that people have energy fields in addition to what they are. The energy field is the *fundamental unit* of the living system and the physical body is but one manifestation of that energy field.
- People are open systems engaged in continuous interaction with the environment.
- When a person is sick, there is an imbalance in the person's energy field.
- When a person uses his or her intent to help or to heal a person, the energy field of the recipient may repattern toward greater wellness. Noncontact therapeutic touch is an example of this. In fact, recent studies have shown that healers working through therapeutic touch have affected biochemical changes in the person being healed.

Therapeutic touch is not massage, but rather a type of therapy wherein a trained healer—often a nurse—with hands placed approximately six or eight inches above the patient's body, practices a sort of choreography with his or her hands, which has the effect of moving heat from one place in the body to another. Bill Moyers's 1993 PBS production, *Healing and the Mind,* showed an effective example of this by a Chinese physician working on a young man with a brain tumor. Therapeutic touch can accelerate wound healing, increase the rate of growth in plants, increase the level of human hemoglobin, can decrease pain, decrease diastolic blood pressure, and decrease anxiety. The technique of therapeutic touch was developed in the early 1970s by Dolores Krieger, a nurse-academician at New York University (NYU), who is said to be able to diagnose a patient's illness without taking a history, just by "feeling" the imbalances through therapeutic touch.

Dr. Martha Rogers, a professor of nursing science at NYU in the 1960s, developed the concept of people interacting with others in the environment via an energy exchange. According to Rogers, "the human field extends beyond the discernible mass we perceive as the body and is coextensive with the environmental energy field." This concept underlies major Eastern philosophies and is also an idea at the cutting edge of modern science.

For those of us reared in a culture that believes in material objects that can be experienced directly through the senses, it takes a huge leap of faith to understand that the human body is not what it appears to be: a solid, tangible mass. Physicists tell us that our bodies are not solid, but that they are comprised of millions of molecules; and beyond that, of atomic particles, spinning around at great speeds, bound together by magnetic forces. But as this is not discernible to the human eye, it takes either a leap of faith or extensive reading of scientific literature to understand this phenomenon of physics. In between all of these molecules that comprise our bodily organs and skeleton and inside our atoms are spaces or voids, and it is through these voids, Deepak Chopra, M.D., tells us, that we are able to communicate with other individuals to heal them or interact with the environment or, on a larger scale, the cosmos. Through the practice of meditation, one is able to achieve a higher level of consciousness to move beyond the thoughts and activities of everyday living to reach and influence other life forms. It's not just people who can be affected by this.

In *Healing Words,* Larry Dossey, M.D., investigates the power of prayer using Daniel Benor's definition of prayer or spiritual healing as "the intentional influence of one or more people upon another living system without utilizing known physical means of intervention." Dr. Dossey explains that prayer can be *directed* (where one specifies the desired outcome) or *non-directed* (one may repeat a phrase such as "thy will be done" or "let it be") with equal effectiveness. Dr. Dossey cites hundreds of studies on fungi, yeast, and bacteria, as well as animals and humans. The following two examples give a sense of the compelling nature of this research.

1. *A group called Spindrift in Salem, Oregon, tested prayer on simple biological systems, such as germinating seeds.* They used non-directed prayer for one group and did nothing for the control group; they later measured the respective germination rates of the seeds and found unequivocally that prayer was effective.

2. *In a study done at the Mind Science Foundation in San Antonio, Texas, researchers studied the ability of 62 people to influence the physiology of 271 subjects who were separated at opposite ends of the building from each other.* The subjects were attached to instruments to measure

their electrodermal activity, which records the activity of the sympathetic part of the autonomic nervous system. The influencers were told to exert either a calming or an activating effect on the subjects, using mental imagery as well as attempts to induce either of these conditions (relaxation or activation) in themselves. In a number of cases, the subject actually perceived the same images as the influencer. For example, the influencer might have used a mental image of vigorously shaking the subject's chair in order to cause an activation response and the subject actually perceived the chair being shaken. This is called "transpersonal imagery." This series of experiments demonstrated, without a doubt, that individuals can influence others' physiology even at a distance and even without the subjects' knowledge.

A number of studies researching the effects of healing on fungi, yeast, or bacteria have yielded similar results. For example, 10 subjects tried to inhibit the growth of fungus cultures in a laboratory through conscious intent by concentrating on them from various distances. Out of a total of 194 culture dishes, 151 showed retarded growth. This study was later repeated with subjects located from one to 15 miles away from the fungus cultures and in 16 out of 16 trials, the growth of the fungus was inhibited.

THE ROLE OF THE BUILT ENVIRONMENT IN HEALING

What role does the built environment play in influencing healing? The setting in which care is given—the treatment environment—is one component of the dynamic process of balance. But the point must be made that there is no magic formula for success; an environment free of environmental stressors, harmonious in every way, will not be healing in the absence of staff who have the right attitude. If they view their job as treating disease, and not the person, the disease may be cured but the individual may not feel healed. However, exceptional staff can function in terrible environments and patients may thrive. To maximize positive outcomes, however, a supportive environment

should be combined with well-trained staff. Many are familiar with the trailblazing Planetree philosophy that has created a quiet revolution in our thinking about appropriate ways to deliver care.

Recently I accompanied my 88-year-old father to a prominent hospital. He was suffering from gangrene in his leg and multiple complications arising from his having only 25 percent heart function. In spite of this, he was in good spirits and optimistic. Within five minutes of placing him in the hospital bed, four nurses and skilled technicians arrived to do a number of invasive procedures such as creating a venous port for starting an IV. At first I was impressed by the sheer number of individuals and what appeared to be proficiency in their respective professional skills.

Hours later, it hit me like a thunderbolt that none of these individuals had introduced herself to me or my father, none of them had made any attempt to hold his hand or touch him, no one had asked his name (and therefore never had addressed him by name); he was just a body needing repair. They treated him in a totally mechanistic manner—as Lee Kaiser describes it, "repairing the car but not thinking about the driver." In fact, it took two days of repeated requests before the nurses found the time to write his name on the signage plaque outside his door and it took 24 hours before they even wristbanded him. Although a well-designed setting is important, probably nothing is more important to a patient's well-being than the attitude of those delivering the care.

Healing environments cannot be achieved by a prescriptive set of design details; what is important is an attitude about delivering healthcare services that is patient-centered: where patients' convenience and comfort are regarded more highly than certain operational issues. The physical setting in a healing environment supports the new patient-centered operational protocols. Patients need access to medical charts and information, and they need to be able to eat when hungry, not at prescribed mealtimes. Families need spaces on the nursing unit where they can feel comfortable and have their needs met.

Nursing units need patient/family kitchens that are residential in character, where a patient in a bathrobe can drink a cup of coffee and read the newspaper, as one might at home. Also important is residential-type lighting, or at least lighting that is indirect. Although one can think of dozens of ways to improve the treatment environment, everything we do is aimed at one specific goal: *to reduce stress.*

PHYSIOLOGY OF STRESS

In 1936, Austrian physician and scientist Hans Selye pioneered a new frontier with his revolutionary discoveries about stress. His research demonstrated that hormones released during stress participate in the development of many degenerative diseases, including brain hemorrhage, hardening of the arteries, coronary thrombosis, certain types of high blood pressure, kidney failure, arthritis, peptic ulcers, and cancer.

His definition of stress refers to *wear and tear on the body resulting from attempts to cope with environmental stressors;* this was a new concept of mental and physical illness. He meticulously documented the enormously complex series of interactions among almost all systems of the body as a reaction to stress. There is irrefutable proof that measurable and highly predictable physiological changes take place as a reaction to psychological and environmental stress. This is the basis for the emerging field of psychoneuroimmunology (PNI).

PNI is a term that refers to the role that emotions play in the origin of physical diseases associated with immunological dysfunctions, especially autoimmune diseases, as well as cancer, infections, and allergies. When people are under stress, their immune systems are more likely to fail.

Stress involves the nervous system and the endocrine (hormonal) system. These two systems provide links between mind and body. What we perceive, think, and how well we cope are all set in motion by messages from the brain to the rest of the body. Our brains are writing a prescription for our bodies every minute of every day. When we feel sad, our bodies produce "sad" chemicals, which affect the functioning of internal organs and eventually suppress the immune system.

Music has been known to have an analgesic or painkilling effect when pleasure centers of the brain stimulate the pituitary gland to release endorphins, the body's natural opiate. Many medical centers have been experimenting with aromatherapy (the inhaling of specific

fragrances) to reduce nausea, decrease the amount of anesthesia need-ed in surgery, decrease pain, and lower blood pressure. Scent activates the limbic system, the emotional center of the brain. It should be noted that practitioners are using essential oils, highly distilled essences of herbs and flowers, quite different from the commercial fragrances marketed to consumers in stores selling products for the skin or bath.

ACCEPTANCE OF ALTERNATIVE THERAPIES

There are, in fact, a whole range of alternative therapies in addition to music and aromatherapy—massage, acupuncture, transcendental medi-tation, art therapy, biofeedback, yoga, herbal medicine, and others—that have gained prominence recently. Although not yet mainstream, these therapies have stimulated enough interest that The National Institutes of Health opened the Office of Alternative Medical Practices in 1993 to study the subject. In this supportive climate, a number of promi-nent physicians who work at some of the nation's most prestigious medical centers have come forward recently to reveal their own posi-tive experiences with alternative therapies as adjuncts to allopathic medicine.

As mentioned before, Bill Moyers's PBS special, *Healing and the Mind,* was an extraordinarily well-produced six-hour documentary that explored Eastern medicine and alternative therapies. There has been a veritable explosion of mind/body research in the past few years, much of it focusing on the immune system. Many researchers think the immune system has a level of sophistication that we are just beginning to understand. It may operate as a sixth sense, detecting elements of the environment that elude the other senses: an exten-sion of the brain in the form of a peripheral receptor organ alerting it to new bodily threats. It is a sensory organ. The distinction is that the phenomena it senses are not in the realm of sight, sound, touch, taste, or smell. The immune system is a sensory system for molecular touch.

Dr. Deepak Chopra tells us that our immune cells are constantly eavesdropping on our internal conversations. Immune cells are think-ing cells, "conscious little beings" like brain cells, equivalent to a circulating nervous system. The human body is not a frozen anatomical structure. It's a river of intelligence and energy and information.

Until recently, in spite of Freud's evidence to the contrary, the orthodox medical community has had difficulty accepting the idea that the mind can contribute to the causation of illness. Throughout most of this century, physicians have viewed the body and mind as separate and distinct components; however, there has been a gradual evolution of viewpoint in that regard. An increasing number of physicians are now recognizing that it is important to treat the whole person, not just the diseased organ system. What makes all this so fascinating is that, after years of focusing on medical technology, physicians are just now starting to explore and appreciate the human body's responses to metaphysical forces—to examine theories hinted at by healers centuries ago.

AVOIDANCE OF ENVIRONMENTAL STRESSORS

As new views evolve about the relationship between stress and illness and the influence of positive attitudes on healing, more emphasis will be placed on the design of the patient care environment. Formal prescriptions for creating a healing environment aren't likely to be found, but it is generally acknowledged that the following items are important:

1. *Noise control*
   - Sound of footsteps in corridor.
   - Slamming doors, clanking latches, dishes on food carts.
   - Loudspeaker paging system.
   - Staff conversations from nurse station or staff lounge.
   - Other patients' televisions, radios.

2. *Air quality*
   - Need for fresh air, solarium, or roof garden.
   - Avoidance of noxious off-gassing from synthetic materials, including certain types of paint.
   - Adequate number of air changes.
   - Avoidance of odiferous cleaning agents.

3. *Thermal comfort*
   - Ability to control room temperature and humidity to suit personal needs.

4. *Privacy*
   - Ability to control view of the outdoors.
   - Ability to control social interaction and/or view of patient in adjacent bed.
   - Secure place for personal belongings.
   - Place to display personal mementos (family photos, get-well cards, flowers).

5. *Light*
   - Full-spectrum, non-glare lighting in patient room, good reading light.
   - Ability to control intensity of light.
   - Window should be low enough for patient to see outdoors while lying in bed.

6. *Views of nature*
   - Views of trees, flowers, mountains, ocean, from patient rooms and lounges is highly significant: regenerative power of nature, always changing, never static.
   - Indoor landscaping.

7. *Color*
   - Careful use of color to create mood, lift spirit, make rooms cheerful.
   - Use in bed linens, bedspreads, gowns, personal hygiene kits, accessories, food trays.

8. *Texture*
   - Introduce textural variety in wall surfaces, floors, ceilings, furniture, fabrics, artwork.

9. *Accommodation for families*
   - Provide a place for family members to make them feel welcome, rather than an intrusion.
   - Provide visitor lounges, sleeper chairs, access to vending machines, telephones, cafeteria.

IMPORTANCE OF NATURE

The past few years have seen tremendous improvement in bringing nature (gardens, water elements, natural light, and sunshine) into hospital lobbies, particularly those having an atrium design, but only in rare instances is nature integrated into nursing units and treatment areas, and that's where patients spend their time. There is considerable research to support the benefits of nature in reducing stress, documented by measuring physiological responses such as brain activity, hormonal secretions, blood pressure, respiration, and muscle tension.

While there are many reasons human beings find comfort and solace in nature, some of these feelings may result from symbolism inherent in nature itself. Water, for example, is associated with baptism and rebirth or purification; flowers express the fragility of life; autumn leaves symbolize the onset of winter or advancing age; stones and rocks express strength, permanence, the ability to withstand stress and the forces of nature which over centuries have worn away and shaped cliffs and rocks; a rainbow may symbolize hope.

Some researchers postulate that our responses to nature relate to our evolutionary past and the role that nature played in our survival. We used to understand the rhythm of the tides and the cycles of the moon and sun, and live in harmony with the natural world. Today we rely on time clocks, deadlines, fax machines, telephones, and other people's expectations to structure our lives. We have little time to notice the natural order of things. Yet people seem drawn to nature. City dwellers in New York escape for weekends to the country: it seems to renew and restore them.

Perhaps the most appealing thing about nature is that it is always changing slightly and never static. The movement of leaves, the ever-changing angle and color of a sunset, wind currents on the ocean, the direction of waves, the sway of a palm tree, the movement of clouds, and the shimmering of sunlight on leaves provide just enough stimulation to prevent boredom. Yet it requires little effort to experience nature and appreciate it.

While there is general agreement that views of nature effect measurable physiological changes, there is evidence that simulated views of nature (as in photomurals or art) may be as effective as the real

90

thing. Dr. Yvonne Clearwater, a senior research psychologist and human factors specialist at NASA Ames Research Center, has conducted a number of these studies. She offers these guidelines based on her research into the connection between visual images and physiology:

- Landscapes are preferred over urban views.
- Views with greater perspective are preferred over close-up views.
- Scenes with animals, buildings, or people are less appropriate.
- The biological relevance of water is clear.

In discussions of "good" hospital design, one often hears references to hospitality design, but I have always found this puzzling. Most hotels are highly monotonous in their repetition of decor and the blandness of their artwork. There is a total lack of personalization in a hotel room, along with generally poor lighting, pillows that are too hard, and mindless artwork. It is hard to effect any changes in the room to meet personal needs. Can a person heal in such a setting? To sum up, research tells us that control and choice are the two most important things to a hospitalized patient, in addition to access to nature.

THE HOSPITAL OF THE FUTURE

When I allow myself to daydream, I imagine a hospital in which nurses and doctors making daily rounds dispense vials of essential oils, carefully matched to patients' needs to balance their minds and bodies. Perhaps lavender for Mr. Smith's migraine; peppermint for a child with asthma; the fragrance of oranges and vanilla for a patient to decrease anxiety the night before open-heart surgery. In addition to this, the physician may prescribe a string quartet, sculpture therapy with clay, an herbal bath in a room with therapeutically colored lights, an hour of watching a wide-screen video of tropical rain forests, and 20 minutes of laughter.

There is a physician who may, through his research, make this a reality. Joel Elkes at the University of Louisville is director of the Arts and Medicine program in the Division of Attitudinal and Behavioral Medicine. He's a psychiatrist, neurochemist, psychopharmacologist, and the former director of psychiatry at Johns Hopkins. He is investigating the possibilities of music, visual arts, dance, drama, and humor, in what he says is the first attempt to research the effects of so many artistic disciplines brought together under a single umbrella in a school of medicine. His dream is to establish the arts as a legitimate therapeutic approach in every branch of medicine from pediatrics to gerontology.

CRITERIA FOR EVALUATING HEALING ENVIRONMENTS

- Involve the five senses: sight, touch, sound, taste, smell.
- Provide a connection with nature: gardens, fountains, ponds, fish, birds, flowers, trees, patios, balconies, daylight, fresh air.
- Avoid environmental stressors: poor air quality, noise, poor lighting, odors, color imbalance, lack of privacy, lack of control over patient environment.
- Provide adequately sized, well-designed workspaces as well as lounges (with daylight) to reduce staff stress.
- Address spiritual issues: embrace the joy of living; restore vitality; concept of a "healing temple."
- Break the institutional grid: strive for variety, differentiation, and delight in the architecture.
- Meet functional requirements (adequate storage for equipment, linen carts, etc., shielded from patients' and visitors' view); access to patient for caregivers; reduce clutter.
- Introduce positive distractions: art, music, entertainment, humor.
- Assess opportunities to empower patients (maximize independence; provide options for control).
- Address psychological issues including ethnic/cultural diversity, personality traits, accommodation for families; how to meet the needs of persons with diverse tastes and experiences (e.g., rural vs. urban, factory worker vs. college professor: do disparate groups have *similar* or *different* needs and expectations?)
- In patient rooms, consider the patient's view while lying in bed (clear sight lines to the window to see daylight and views; what do

patients see on the ceiling and the footwall?). Provide amenities, such as a small refrigerator, a place for toiletries at the sink, a tackable surface for mounting greeting cards or family photos, shelves for flowers and plants, a wardrobe, and a place for a family member to sleep.

Jain Malkin is president of Jain Malkin, Inc., an interior architecture firm based in San Diego, California, specializing in healthcare facilities. Malkin has lectured widely and written numerous articles on the psychological effects of healthcare environments. She has taught medical space planning, as well as workshops on creating healing environments at Harvard University's Graduate School of Design in Cambridge, Massachusetts. Malkin is the author of several books, including Medical and Dental Space Planning for the 1990s *and* Hospital Interior Architecture.

CHAPTER REFERENCES AND SOURCES

CHAPTER 1
COLOR THEORY REVISITED

Chart Design

Glenn Ruga, Visual Communications, 47 East Street, Hadley, MA 01035; 413/586-2415.

Product Sources

Color Aid Corporation, 37 East 18th Street, New York, NY 10003; tel. 212/673-5500; fax 212/476-0315.

References

Albers, Joseph. *Interaction of Color.* New Haven: Yale University Press, 1963.

Itten, Johannes. *The Elements of Color.* Edited and with a foreword and evaluation by Faber Birren. New York: Van Nostrand Reinhold, 1970.

CHAPTER 2
COLOR AS LIGHT AND ENERGY

References

Babbit, Edwin. *The Principles of Light and Color.* Secaucus, NJ: Citadel Press, 1967.

Chevreul, M.E. *The Principles of Harmony and the Contrast of Colors.* New York: Reinhold, 1967.

Fischer, Joey. "The Many Possibilities of Art for Health." *Journal of Healthcare Design 3* (1991): 196–199.

Gilbert, Susan. "Harnessing the Power of Light." *New York Times Magazine.* April 26, 1992.

Lieberman, Jacob. *Light — Medicine of the Future.* Santa Fe, NM: Bear & Co., 1991.

Torrice, Antonio, and Ro Logrippo, *In My Room.* New York: Ballantine Books, 1989.

CHAPTER 3
USING FULL-SPECTRUM COLOR
IN INTERIOR SPACES

Artists

Joseph DiGiorgio, 269 Bowery, New York, NY 10002; 212/260-3865.

Diana Kurz, 152 Wooster Street, New York, NY 10012; 212/260-3677.

Laurie Zagon, 2700 Woodlands Village, Suite 300-176, Flagstaff, AZ 86001; 602/774-1620.

Photography

Jim Koch Photography, 1723 Irvine Avenue, Newport Beach, CA 92660; 714/957-5719.

Leda Moser, c/o Joseph DiGiorgio, 269 Bowery, New York, NY 10002; 212/260-3865.

Kevin Noble, 51 Murray Street #5, New York, NY 10007; 212/285-9202.

Product Sources

AlliedSignal Fibers, P.O. Box 31, Petersburg, VA 23804; 804/520-3306.

Avonite, 1945 Highway 304, Belen, NM 97002; 505/864-3800.

BASF, Fibers Division, P.O. Box Drawer D, Williamsburg, VA 23187; 804/887-6573.

DuPont Company, Fabricated Products Department, Room B-11210, Market Street, Wilmington, DE 19898; 800/527-2601.

DuPont Corian. Chestnut Run Plaza #702, Wilmington, DE 19880-0702; 800/426-7426.

DuPont Flooring Systems, Walnut Run, Room 1049, Wilmington, DE 19880-0722; 302/999-5560.

Formica Corporation, 10155 Reading Road, Cincinnati, OH 45241; 513/786-3400.

Monsanto Company/Fibers Division, 1460 Broadway, New York, NY 10036; 212/382-9600.

Wilsonart, 600 General Bruce Drive, Temple, TX 76504; 817/778-2711.

References

"Lighting Affects Children's Growth, Health, and Achievement." *Environmental Design Research Association Newsletter 26,* No. 4 (1993): 11.

Coates, Gary, and Susan Siepl-Coates. "Vidarkliniken: A Study of the Anthroposophical Healing Center in Jarna, Sweden." Paper read at the Built Form and Culture Research Conference, Arizona State University, Tempe, Arizona, 1989. (Available from Gary Coates, Department of Architecture, 211 Seaton Hall, Manhattan, KS 66506-2901; 913/532-5953.)

Gappell, Millicent. "Design Technology: Psychoneuroimmunology." *Journal of Healthcare Design* 4 (1992): 127-130.

Kaufman, Donald, and Taffy Dahl. *Color: Natural Palettes for Painted Rooms.* New York: Clarkson/Potter, 1992.

Nightingale, Florence. 1888. *Notes on Nursing.*

Ulrich, Roger. "Effects of Interior Design on Wellness: Theory and Recent Scientific Research." *Journal of Healthcare Design* 3 (1991): 97-109.

CHAPTER 4
PROJECT EXAMPLES: HOSPITALITY, LABORATORIES, OFFICES, SCHOOLS

Chart Design

Glenn Ruga, Jennifer Getzin/Visual Communications, 47 East Street, Hadley, MA 01035; 413/586-2415.

Design Firms

DiLeonardo International, Inc., 2350 Post Road, Warwick, RI 02886; 401/732-2900.

Griswold, Heckel & Kelly (GHK) Associates, Inc., 55 West Wacker Drive, Suite 600, Chicago, IL 60601-1611; 312/263-6605.

Interior Space International (ISI), 305 E. 46th Street, New York, NY 10017; 212/751-0800.

Lescher and Mahoney, 2141 East Camelback Road, Suite 100, Phoenix, AZ 85016-4712; 602/381-8580.

Lord Aeck & Sargent, 1201 Peachtree Street NE, 400 Colony Square, Suite 300, Atlanta, GA 30361; 404/872-0330.

Mekus Johnson, Inc., 455 E. Illinois, Chicago, IL 60611; 312/661-0778.

Jordan Mozer & Associates Ltd., 228 W. Illinois, Chicago, IL 60610; 312/661-0060.

NBBJ Architects, 111 S. Jackson Street, Seattle, WA 98104; 206/223-5555.

Ross Barney+Jankowski, Inc., 11 E. Adams Street, Suite 700, Chicago, IL 60603; 312/663-5220.

The Steinberg Group, Architects, 60 Pierce Avenue, San Jose, CA 95110; 408/295-5446.

STUDIOS Architecture, 99 Green Street, San Francisco, CA 94111; 415/398-7575.

Photographers

Dennis Andersen Photography, 200 Gate 5 Road, Suite 117, Sausalito, CA 94965; 415/332-7438.

Wayne Cable Photography, 401 West Superior, 2nd Floor, Chicago, IL 60610; 312/951-1799.

Tom Crane Photography, 113 Cumberland Place, Bryn Mawr, PA 19010; 215/525-2444.

Jonathan Hillyer Photography Inc., 2604 Parkside Drive N.E., Atlanta, GA 30305; 404/841-6679.

Steve Hall, Marco Lorenzetti, Jon Miller/Hedrich-Blessing, 11 West Illinois Street, Chicago, IL 60610; 312/321-1151.

Chas McGrath Photography, 3735 Kansas Drive, Santa Rosa, CA 95405; 707/545-5853.

Sharon Risedorph Photography, 761 Clementina, San Francisco, CA 94103; 415/431-5851.

Dave Tate Photography, Box 2815, Sedona, AZ 86339; 602/282-1822.

Paul Warchol Photography, 144 Mulberry, New York, NY 10013; 212/431-3461.

CHAPTER 5
PROJECT EXAMPLES: HEALTHCARE

Chart Design

Glenn Ruga, Jennifer Getzin/Visual Communications, 47 East Street, Hadley, MA 01035; 413/586-2415.

Design Firms

Eric Asmussen, Jarna, Sweden

Ellerbe Becket, 800 LaSalle Avenue, Minneapolis, MN 55402; 612/376-2426.

98

Martha Child Interiors, 904 Douglass Drive, McLean, VA 22101; 703/356-9650.

HKS Architects, 700 N. Pearl, Suite 1100, Dallas, TX 75201; 214/969-5599.

Jain Malkin Inc., 7855 Fay Avenue, Suite 100, La Jolla, CA 92037; 619/454-3377.

NBBJ Architects, 111 S. Jackson Street, Seattle, WA 98104; 206/223-5555.

Pasanella + Klein Stolzman + Berg, 330 West 42nd Street, New York, NY 10036; 212/594-2010.

Rios Associates, 8008 West Third, Los Angeles, CA 90048; 213/852-6717.

Craig Roeder Associates, 3829 North Hall Street, Dallas, TX 72219; 214/528-2300.

TRO/The Ritchie Organization, 80 Bridge Street, Newton, MA 02158; 617/969-9400.

Photography

Peter Aaron/ESTO Photographics, 222 Valley Place, Mamaroneck, NY 10543; 914/698-4060.

Chuck Choi Architectural Photography, 204 Berkeley Place, Brooklyn, NY 11217; 718/638-5825.

Robt. Ames Cook Architectural Photography, 828 Neely's Chase Drive, Madison, TN 37115; 615/865-6648.

David Hewitt/Anne Garrison Architectural Photography, 2387 Seaside Street, San Diego, CA 92107; 619/222-4036.

Warren Jagger Photography Inc., 150 Chestnut Street, Providence, RI 02906; 401/351-7366.

Skip Meachen, 101 Mathews Point North, Hilton Head, SC 29926; 803/681-2918.

Steve McClelland Photography, 4990 Dick Street, San Diego, CA 92115; 619/582-9812.

Dennis Moch Photography, 13715 Sparren Avenue, San Diego, CA 92129; 619/538-0236.

Max Plunger, Maltesholmsvagen 154, 16562 Hasselby, Sweden; 011 46 8 4718090.

References

Arditi, A., and K. Knoblauch. "Choosing Effective Display Color for the Partially-Sighted." Technical report published by The Lighthouse Research Institute, New York, 1994.

Linn, Charles. "Color It Healthy." *Architectural Record Lighting* (August 1993): 26–31.

Roeder, Craig. "High, Higher, Highest." *Lighting Design and Application* (March 1993): 22–24.

FURTHER READING

RECOMMENDED BOOKS
ON COLOR AND LIGHT

Amber, Reuben. *Color Therapy.* Santa Fe, NM: Aurora Press, 1983.

Considered "new age," this book offers interesting information on the physiological aspects of color in relation to healing. It is useful for studying the physical, emotional, and spiritual findings on color.

Birren, Faber. *Color Psychology and Color Therapy.* Citadel Press, 1950.

One of the most important works by Birren, in the United States the foremost authority on the visual, physiological, and psychological responses to color from the 1950s until his death in 1988. This book introduced the idea of color psychology as a useful tool for design professionals and manufacturers.

Birren, Faber. *Light, Color and Environment.* New York: Van Nostrand Reinhold, 1982.

Birren's last book explores not only the psychological effects of color, but also the physiological effects and how they relate to health and well-being.

Gimbel, Theo. *Healing Through Colour.* Safron Walden, England: C.W. Daniel Company Ltd., 1980.

Another new age book, this one has an interesting chapter on light and color as a science, as well as a chapter on how to treat illness with color.

Hollwich, Fritz. *The Influence of Ocular Light Perception on Metabolism in Man and Animal.* New York: Springer-Verlag, 1979.

An important work on the physical and chemical effects of light in humans and animals.

Hope, A., and M. Walch. *The Color Compendium.* New York: Van Nostrand Reinhold, 1990.

A comprehensive dictionary of color terms, historical facts, and individuals who have made significant contributions to the study and use of color.

Le Clair, Charles. *Color in Contemporary Painting: Integrating Practice and Theory.* New York: Watson Guptill, 1991.

A good art book that offers information on color theory principles, as well as an abundance of work by acclaimed artists who are noted colorists (including the author, who was dean of the Tyler School of Art in Philadelphia for many years). It offers a good explanation of how form and color are used in contemporary art.

Liberman, Jacob. *Light: Medicine of the Future.* Santa Fe, NM: Bear & Company, 1991.

Perhaps the first book that explains the science and spiritual relationship of healing with light. Chapter 1 discusses the sun as the natural rhythm of life and explains the relationship of color and light as a healing tool.

Linton, Harold. *Color Forecasting: A Survey of International Color Marketing.* New York: Van Nostrand Reinhold, 1994.

Features a wealth of information through essays written by some of the world's most well-known color forecasters and consultants. It is the best book to date on understanding forecasting and color marketing, particularly in regard to methods for creating color trends.

Mahnke, Frank H., and Rudolph H. Mahnke. *Color and Light in Manmade Environments.* New York: Van Nostrand Reinhold, 1987.

Offers advice on how color and light, when used correctly, can improve different types of environments, including the workplace and healthcare facilities.

Marberry, Sara O. *Color in the Office.* New York: Van Nostrand Reinhold, 1993.

Analyzes color and design trends from the 1950s to the 1990s and offers a generous display of color photos from these periods.

Mella, Dorothee L. *The Language of Color.* Warner Books, 1988.

A fun and interesting look at the psychological responses of humans to color, including a color test of personal preferences.

Moore-Ede, M.C., F.M. Slzman, and C.A. Fuller. *The Clocks That Time Us.* Cambridge, MA: Harvard University Press, 1982.

Fascinating reading on circadian rhythms, the behavioral and physiological effects of the 24-hour cycle of the earth's rotation on human beings.

Steiner, Rudolph. *Colour.* London: Rudolph Steiner Press, 1971.

A small, pocket-size book by a German philosopher, scientist, and educator, that explores the art, spirit, and energy of color as it relates to the laws of nature.

Theroux, Alexander. *The Primary Colors: Three Essays.* New York: Henry Holt, 1994.

Wonderful color imagery by novelist and poet Theroux, whose perceptions evoke emotions and feelings that can further clarify the human response to color.

Torrice, Antonio F., and Ro Logrippo. *In My Room.* New York: Ballantine Books, 1989.

A landmark work on designing interiors for children, based on the late Torrice's work with color. Interesting reading on the healing properties of color and color as electromagnetic energy.

Venolia, Carol. *Healing Environments: Your Guide to Indoor Well-Being.* Berkeley, CA: Celestial Arts, 1988.

Written in a simple and straightforward style, this book offers information on the psychological meanings of the spectrum colors, as well as aspects of healing environments, including the thermal environment, sound and noise, indoor air quality, and plants and gardens.

Winfree, Arthur. T. *The Timing of Biological Clocks.* New York, NY: Scientific American Library, 1987.

An important work by one of the world's foremost theoreticians on circadian rhythms. The passage of cyclic time is explored and illustrated by the additive color system, which links color, light, and circadian rhythms.

Wood, Betty. *The Healing Power of Color.* Destiny Books, 1985.

Although some of the concepts presented in this new age book have now been validated by scientific research, it does not offer any documentation on the healing power of color. Nonetheless, it does still provide thought-provoking information.

ADDITIONAL ARTICLES AND PAPERS ON COLOR AND LIGHT RESEARCH

Ainsworth, R., L. Simpson, and D. Cassell. "Effects of Three Colors in an Office Interior on Mood and Performance." *Perceptual and Motor Skills* 76, No. 1 (February 1993): 235.

Baldell, M.V., I. Toschi, M. Motta, and A. Ascari. "The Importance of Color and Shape in the Vision of the Elderly." *Archives of Gerontology Geriatrics* 12 (suppl. 2, 1991): 119-122.

Beral, V., et al. "Malignant Melanoma and Exposure to Fluorescent Light at Work." *Lancet* 2 (1982): 406-418.

Biological Rhythms: Implications for the Worker. U.S. Government Printing Office. OTA-BA-463 (1991): 1–249

Brainard, G.C., J.R. Gaddy, F.M. Barker, J.P. Hanifin, and M.D. Rollag. "Mechanisms in the Eye That Mediate the Biological and Therapeutic Effects of Light in Humans." In *Light and Biological Rhythms in Man* 63, edited by L. Wetterberg. Pergamon Press, Stockholm, Sweden (1993): 29–53.

Brainard, G.C., R.R. Long, J.P Hanifin, F.L. Ruberg, J.R. Gaddy, C.A. Bernecker, F.J. Fernsler, and M.D. Rollag. "Architectural Lighting: Balancing Biological Effects with Utility Costs." In *The Biological*

Effects of Light, edited by M.F. Holick and E.G. Jung. Walter de Gruyter & Co., New York (1994): 169–185.

Brainard, G.C., N.E. Rosenthal, D. Sherry, R.G. Skwerer, M. Waxler, and D. Kelly. "Effects of Different Wavelengths in Seasonal Affective Disorder." *Journal of Affective Disorders* 20, No. 4 (1990): 209–216.

Cooper, B., C. Gowland, and J. McIntosh. "The Use of Color in the Environment of the Elderly to Enhance Function." *Clinics in Geriatric Medicine* 2, No. 1 (February 1986): 151–163.

Cooper, B., M. Ward, C. Gowland, and J. McIntosh. "The Use of the Lanthony New Color Test in Determining the Effects of Aging on Color Vision." *Journal of Gerontology. Psychological Sciences* 46, No. 6 (1991): 320-324.

Engelman, R. "Light Kills AIDS Virus in Blood." *Scripps Howard News Service.* January 13, 1988.

Fleming, J., S. Holmes, and L. Barton. "Differences in Color Preferences of School Age Children in Varying Stages of Health: A Preliminary Study." *Maternal and Child Nursing* 17, No. 3 (1988): 173–189.

Graverholz, J. "SDI Lasers Inactivate the AIDS Virus: An Interview With Lester Mathews, Ph.D." *Science and Technology EIR.* (January 29, 1988).

Hiatt, L. "Color and Use of Color in Environments for Older People." *Nursing Homes* 30, No. 3 (1981): 18–22.

Hood, C.M., and E.F. Faye. "Evaluating the Living Situation." *The Aging Eye and Low Vision.* Lighthouse National Center for Vision and Aging. The Lighthouse Inc., New York (1992): 46–54.

Hughes, P.C. *Natural Light and the Psychobiological System of Man.* CIE Publication 562 (1983).

Joki, M.V. "The Psychological Effects on Man of Air Movement and the Colour of His Surroundings." *Applied Ergonomics* (June 1984): 119–125.

Keister, E., Jr. "Living Without Light." *Science Illustrated*. (March/April 1989): 26–32.

Kuyller, Rikard, and Carin Lindsten. "Health and Behavior of Children in Classrooms With and Without Windows." *Journal of Environmental Psychology* 12 (1992): 305–317.

Lewy, A.J., et al. "Light Suppresses Melatonin Secretion in Humans." *Science* 210 (1989): 1267–1269.

Liberman, Jacob. "The Effect of Syntonic Colored Light: Stimulation on Certain Visual and Cognitive Functions." *Journal of Optometric Vision Development* 17 (June 1986).

Maas, J.B., et al. "Effects of Spectral Difference in Illumination on Fatigue." *Journal of Applied Psychology* 59 (1974): 524–526.

Marshall, John. "Light and the Aging Eye." *The RSA Journal 138*. No.5406 (May 1990): 406–418.

Martin, Charlotte. "Interior Design for Hospitals: Preferences of Patients and Staff for Color in the Patient Room Environment." Ph.D. dissertation, Oklahoma State University, 1992.

Moore-Ede, M.C., C.A. Czeisler, and G.S. Richardson. "Circadian Timekeeping in Health and Disease." Part I: "Basic Properties of Circadian Pacemakers." *New England Journal of Medicine* 309 (1983): 469-476. Part II: "Clinical Implications of Circadian Rhythmicity." *New England Journal of Medicine* 309 (1983): 530–536.

Ott, John "Color and Light: Their Effects on Plants, Animals, and People, Part 1." *Journal of Biosocial Research* 7, 1985.

Pitts, D.G. "The Effects of Aging on Selected Visual Functions: Dark Adaptation, Visual Acuity, Stereopsia, and Brightness Contrast." In *Aging and Human Visual Function*. Modern Aging Research, vol. 2, edited by R. Sekulor, D. Kline, and K. Diamukes. 1982, 131–160.

Rigel, D.S., et al. "Malignant Melanoma and Exposure to Fluorescent Light at Work." *Lancet* 1 (1983): 704.

Schauss, A. "The Physiological Effect of Color on the Suppression of Human Aggression: Research on Baker-Miller Pink." *International Journal of Biosocial Research* 7, No. 1 (1985): 65–64.

Smith, R.C. "Light and Health, a Broad Overview." *Lighting Design + Application* (February 1986).

Tideiksaar, R. "Avoiding Falls." *The Aging Eye and Low Vision.* Lighthouse National Center for Vision and Aging. The Lighthouse, Inc., New York (1992): 55-60.

U.S. Government Printing Office. *Biological Rhythms: Implications for the Worker.* OTA-BA-463 (1991): 1–249.

Whitfield, T., and T. Wilshire. "Color Psychology: A Critical Review." *Genetic, Social and General Psychology Monographs.* (1990): 387–411.

Wise, B.K., and J. Wise. *The Human Factors of Color in Environmental Design: A Critical Review.* Study done by the Department of Psychology. Seattle, Washington, 1987.

Wohlfarth, H., and S.C. Wohlfarth. "The Effect of Color Psychodynamic Environmental Modification upon Psychophysiological and Behavioral Reactions of Severely Handicapped Children." *The International Journal of Biosocial Research* 3, No. 1. (1982): 10–38.

Wurtman, R.J. "The Effects of Light on Man and Other Mammals." *Annual Review of Physiology* 37 (1975): 467–483.

INDEX

Abstract expressionism, 4
Albers, Josef, 4
Allied, 20
Ambulatory care facility projects, 36
anthroposophy, 20
Apple Learning Center, 30
Asmussen, Erik, 20
Avonite, 20

Babbit, Edwin, 12, 14
BASF Fibers, 20
Bauhaus School, 3,4
Big Park Elementary School, 33
Black Mountain College, 4
Burger King Corporate World
    Headquarters, 30

Callaway, Fuller E., Jr., Manufacturing
    Research Center, 28
Casa Palmera Care Center, 42
Cesar Chavez Elementary School, 32
Chevreul, M. E., 3, 15
Chopra, Deepak, 50, 54
Coates, Gary and Susanne, 21
Color:
    human response to, 16
    measurement of, 22
    use in healthcare environments,
      35–36, 56, 69

Color-Aid paper, 5
Color and light:
    Kirlian photography, 14
    relationship, 11
    spectrum, 11
    visual interpretation of, 15
Color theory:
    history of, 3–5
    principles of, 5–9
Columbia Presbyterian Medical Center,
    42, 43
Cypress Club, 28

Dahl, Taffy, 20
Davis, Mikol, 14
Day care project, 37
DiGiorgio, Joseph, 24
Dossey, Larry, 50
DuPont, 20

Fischer, Joey, 11
Formica, 20
Full-spectrum color:
    artwork, 23–25
    benefits of using, 16, 17
    common mistakes, 21
    hotel and restaurant projects, 27, 28
    laboratory project, 28, 29
    light fixtures, 22, 23
    lighting studies, 12, 13, 22, 23, 72–75

materials and finishes, 19–21
next steps, 45, 46
office projects, 29–31
palette development, 19–21, 22, 23, 27
planning checklist, 25
school projects, 32, 33

Gappell, Millicent, 22
Goethe, 3
Gropius, Walter, 3, 4

Healing:
    alternative therapies, 54, 55
    role of built environment, 51–53
Healing environments:
    accommodation for families, 56
    air quality, 55
    aromatherapy, 53, 54
    artwork, 47, 48
    color, 56
    criteria for evaluating, 59, 60
    definition of, 47, 48
    importance of nature, 57, 58
    light, 56
    music, 53, 56
    noise control, 55
    patient-centered care, 52
    privacy, 56
    stress, 53, 54
    texture, 56
    thermal comfort, 56
    views of nature, 56–58
HealthPark Medical Center, 38, 40, 41
Hollwich, Fritz, 12, 70
Hospital projects, 38–41

Institute of Noetic Sciences, 48
Itten, Johannes, 3, 4
    seven color contrasts, 8

Journal of Healthcare Design, 47

Kaiser, Lee, 52
Kandinsky, Wassily, 3
Karrington on the Scioto, 42
Kaufman, Donald, 20
Kirlian photography, 14
Klee, Paul, 3
Krippner, Stanley, 14
Kurz, Diana, 24

Lazur painting, 21
Liberman, Jacob, 11, 70
Light:
    activation of biological clock, 11
    behavioral patterns, 11
    circadian rhythms, 11, 12
    daylight, 22
    electromagnetic spectrum, 13, 14
    healing effects of, 11–13
    quality, 29
    use in healing environments, 65
Lighthouse Research Institute, 35
Long-term care projects, 42

Malkin, Jain, 47–60, 66
Marshall O'Toole Gerstein Murray & Borun, 30
Mattel Child Development Center, 37
Mayo Clinic, 39
Medical office project, 42, 43
Mind/body research:
    energy fields, 49, 50
    immune system, 54, 55
    meditation, 50
    PBS television special, 49, 54
    spiritual healing, 50, 51
    stress, 35
Monsanto, 20
Moyers, Bill, 49, 54

INDEX

NASA, 13, 58
National Institute of Mental Health, 13
National Institutes of Health, 54
Nature, 3, 56–58
Newton, Sir Isaac, 11
Nightingale, Florence, 23

Ott, John, 12

Patwin Elementary School, 33
Planetree philosophy, 52
Price Waterhouse, 31
psychoneuroimmunology, 53

Ramada Renaissance Hotel, 27
Roeder, Craig, 38, 40, 41, 66

San Diego Children's Hospital and
    Health Center, 38

Schopenhauer, 3
Scripps Memorial Hospital, 36
Seasonal Affective Disorder, 13
Simon Marketing, 31
Sixth Symposium on Healthcare
    Design, 47
St. Francis Hospital, 36, 37

Third Symposium on Healthcare
    Design, 11
Torrice, Antonio, 14, 71

Ulrich, Roger, 23, 24

Vidarkliniken, 20, 21, 39

Wilsonart, 20

Zagon, Laurie 24, 25